CHARISMS AND CHARISMATIC RENEWAL

Charisms and Charismatic Renewal

A Biblical and Theological Study

Francis A. Sullivan, S.J.

SERVANT BOOKS
Ann Arbor, Michigan

Published by Servant Books
P.O. Box 8617
Ann Arbor, Michigan 48107

Book Design by John B. Leidy

Scripture quotations are from the *Revised Standard Version of the Bible*, copyrighted 1946, 1952 © 1971, 1973; *The New American Bible*, copyright © 1970 by the Confraternity of Christian Doctrine, Washington, D.C., all rights reserved; *The New English Bible*, copyright © 1961, 1970, the delegates of the Oxford University Press and the syndics of the Cambridge University Press. Printed in the United States of America

ISBN 0-89283-121-9

Contents

Foreword

UNDER THE TITLE *Charisms and Charismatic Renewal* this book offers a series of clarifications in a field which, despite numerous popular treatments, has up to now been left relatively uncultivated from the point of view of Catholic theology, both systematic and pastoral. In the pentecostal world there are many publications, giving interpretations with which we often cannot agree. We Catholics are lagging seriously behind in this respect. This book comes at the right time. Indeed, I would say that it was more than time to integrate a theology of the charisms into a total, sacramental vision of the church, and thus to give to the renewal its theological credentials.

At the Council we underlined the importance and the perennially up-to-date character of the charismatic aspect of the church. But at that time no one suspected that shortly after the Council, the charismatic renewal was going to prolong, as it were, the effectiveness of the Council, and cause us to experience "a kind of new Pentecost" (to borrow the expression of John XXIII). Nothing is more important than clarity in this delicate area of the charisms, starting with clarity of terminology. A Chinese wise man, being asked, "What would you do if you were master of the world?" replied, "I would restore the meaning of words." A reply that has far-reaching implications.

The author has a personal charism of clarity and clarification—a rare gift—which he has exercised with a magnificent sense of nuance and balance, along with care to give the proper weight to all the elements needed for a synthetic view of the whole. Among the different exegetical hypotheses, he has chosen the ones that will no doubt obtain the widest consensus.

I find in these pages another gift of the Spirit, that of humility, which prompts the author to treat with moderation and fairness those with whose opinions he does not agree. No one can feel that he has been misconstrued, even if he has been contradicted, but each can find himself enriched by Father Sullivan's observations. I find his approach ecumenical, serene, and constructive.

I wish to thank Father Sullivan, on behalf of the charismatic renewal, for the work he has accomplished in these pages, and to express my hope that he will continue his research in other similar studies. In this way he will contribute to the dismantling of prejudices and to the acceptance of a movement of the Spirit that is spreading through the six continents, a movement that is rich in hope for the future, if people recognize and grasp the grace that is being offered now.

I am convinced that the renewal, rightly understood, can renew the church of God in a great many ways.

Léon Joseph Cardinal Suenens

ONE

Charisms and Charismatic Renewal

THE WORDS "charism" and "charismatic" are in such common use among Catholics today that it is hard to realize that they were so unfamiliar to most of us less than twenty years ago. I have a personal recollection which brings this home to me in a very vivid way. In the fall of 1963, the bishops at the second session of Vatican II were discussing the draft of the Constitution on the Church. This draft included a paragraph on "the charisms of the faithful."[1] From time to time the American bishops would meet to discuss the issues due to come up in the Council, and they would usually invite a theologian to give them his ideas on the issue and respond to their questions about it. It happened that I was the theologian asked to give the presentation on the question of the charisms.

At that time I had been teaching the course on the church at the Gregorian University for about six years. And I have to confess that this was the first time I had ever prepared a lecture on the charisms of the faithful. I am quite sure that I was not the only Catholic ecclesiologist of that period of whom the same would have been true. Indeed, the lack of attention to the charisms in Catholic theology was brought home to me even more vividly when, in preparation for my lecture to the bishops, I went to consult the standard encyclopedias of Catholic theology. To my astonishment, I found that there was no article on the charisms in the prestigious *Dictionnaire de Théologie Catholique*!

The consultation of other Catholic encyclopedias was more rewarding, but at the same time led me to realize that there were two quite different notions of "charism" current in Catholic theology. According to the article by X. Ducros in the *Dictionnaire de Spiritualité,* charisms are extraordinary gifts of grace, such as one might expect to find in the lives of saints and mystics.[2] A. Lemonnyer, author of the article on charisms in the *Dictionnaire de la Bible, Supplément,* draws quite a different notion of the charisms from an analysis of the teaching of St. Paul.[3] According to this view, charisms are gifts of grace which equip people for the roles and ministries which they are to have in the body of Christ. Some of these gifts and ministries are extraordinary, but many are not; they are distributed widely among the members of the body, as each member is intended to make some contribution to the life of the whole body. Briefly, one can express these two different notions of "charism" by saying that the first sees charisms as rare and extraordinary gifts of grace, while the second sees charisms as useful gifts that equip even ordinary people for various kinds of service in the body of Christ.

Inevitably, these two differing views were reflected in the discussion of the paragraph on charisms during the second session of the Council, in October, 1963. The first of these views was championed by Cardinal Ruffini, who strongly objected to the notion that in our day many of the faithful are gifted with charisms, and that such people can be relied on to make a significant contribution to the upbuilding of the church. On the contrary, he argued, such gifts today "are extremely rare and altogether exceptional."[4] In Cardinal Ruffini's opinion, it is obvious that charisms have no important role to play in the life of the modern church.

Six days later, Cardinal Suenens replied, in a speech that has been widely read, since it was published in a volume of Council speeches.[5] For Suenens, the charisms are no "peripheral or accidental phenomenon in the life of the Church"; on the contrary, they are "of vital importance for the building up of the mystical body."[6] While it is true that in the time of St. Paul some charismatic gifts were dramatic and surprising, "we should never think that the gifts of the Spirit are exclusively and principally in these phenomena which are rather extraordinary and uncommon."[7] Nor are the charisms the privilege of a few; rather, "every Christian, educated or simple, has his gift in his daily life. . . . Does not each and every one of us here know of laymen and laywomen in his own diocese who are truly called by God? They are endowed by the Spirit with various charisms in the fields of catechetics, evangelization, apostolic action in all its ramifications, in social work and charitable activity. . . . Without these charisms, the ecclesiastical ministry would be impoverished and sterile."[8] In conclusion, Cardinal Suenens proposed that the charisms be given a greater emphasis in the Council's treatment of the church as the People of God.

In the end, Cardinal Suenens' view was the one that prevailed at the Council. His proposal that the charisms be given greater emphasis was also ratified, when the Council approved an emendation suggested by Bishop McEleney of Kingston, Jamaica, for the strengthening and clarification of the conciliar statement about the charismatic gifts.[9] The amended text became what is now the second paragraph of no. 12 of the Constitution on the Church. The following is my translation of this text.

It is not only through the sacraments and official ministries that the Holy Spirit sanctifies and leads the People of God and enriches it with virtues. Granting his gifts "to each one as he chooses" (1 Cor 12:11), he also distributes special graces among the faithful of every rank, by which he makes them able and willing to undertake various tasks or services advantageous for the renewal and upbuilding of the church, according to the words of the Apostle: "To each is given the manifestation of the Spirit for a useful purpose" (1 Cor 12:7). These charisms, whether they be the more unusual or the more simple and widely diffused, are to be received with thanksgiving and consolation, for they are exceedingly suitable and useful for the needs of the church. At the same time, extraordinary gifts are not to be rashly sought after, nor are the fruits of apostolic labor to be presumptuously expected from them. In any case, judgment as to their genuineness and proper use belongs to those who preside in the church, upon whom especially falls the obligation not to extinguish the Spirit, but to test all things and hold fast to that which is good (cf. 1 Thes 5:19-21).[10]

Let us look at this text in detail, to see how the Council wishes us to understand the nature and function of the charisms. It describes them as "special graces by which he makes people able and willing to undertake various tasks or services." Such gifts are not the privilege of any class of people in the church, but are "distributed among the faithful of every rank." The term "faithful" here obviously includes all members of the church, from the simplest lay person to the pope. Some of these gifts may be rare and extraordinary, but others are simple and widely diffused. But they are all called "special graces."

The conciliar text suggests two reasons for speaking of charisms as "special graces"; the *way* these gifts are given, and the *purpose* for which they are given. The *way* is special, because it involves a direct intervention of the Holy Spirit in the life of the church. The Council distinguishes between the way the Holy Spirit works "through the sacraments and official ministries," and the way he works in distributing his charismatic gifts. The latter is an immediate intervention of the Spirit, in which he exercises his sovereign freedom to allot his gifts as he wills and to whomever he wills, in a way that cannot be foreseen or controlled by man. Such gifts are "special" also by reason of the purpose for which they are given. Unlike the gifts of faith, hope, and love, which are inseparable from the gift of the indwelling Spirit, and which everyone must have in order to be pleasing to God, the charisms are "distributed among the faithful"; there is no one of these gifts that everyone must have. Their purpose, as described by the Council, is to make people "able and willing to undertake various tasks or services advantageous for the renewal and upbuilding of the Church." In other words, they are specific gifts of grace which equip people for specific kinds of service. Obviously, love is the basic gift which is the indispensable motive force behind any and every genuine service to others. Without love, as St. Paul reminded the Corinthians, even the apparently most generous and heroic gestures of service would be worthless.[11] So we can say that every charism presupposes the gift of love, which moves the person to employ his or her gift in loving service to others. But a charism is a "special grace," in the sense that it equips a person in a particular way for a particular kind of service. As the conciliar text says, it makes people both "able and willing" (*aptos et promptos*). A charism, then, as understood by Vatican II, can be described as a grace-given capacity and willingness for some kind of service that contributes to the renewal and upbuilding of the church.

I think it is important to distinguish between the charism as such, and the charismatic activity in which it is exercised. The charism as such is a gift of grace; it is the grace-factor that enters into the charismatic activity. But it will not be the only component of this activity. In every case the gift of grace will presuppose, build upon, and perfect the natural capacities that are already present. The "special grace," which is the charism as such, will add some new capacity and a new readiness to undertake the activity for which it is given. Because of this grace-factor, the activity can rightly be described as "charismatic." But it will also involve the person's natural gifts and talents.

Just what kind of new capacity the charism will add to one's natural abilities will of course depend on the nature of the charismatic activity for which it is given. For instance, in a given case the charism for teaching may add little to a person's natural capacity to teach, but it will at least add a new willingness to employ this capacity in the service of the people of God, and will probably also add a new effectiveness in teaching with conviction in matters of faith. Other charisms, such as healings and miracles, will obviously add a great deal to the natural capacities of the person who is used as the instrument of such gifts.

From the description of charisms as "special graces," it

follows that charisms cannot be simply identified with natural talents, even though one's natural talents will inevitably enter into the charismatic activity. While gifts of grace and natural talents are both gifts of God, they are different kinds of gifts that come to us in different ways. We inherit our talents from our parents; we do not inherit grace.

The teaching of Vatican II on the charisms of the faithful, while it marks a break with a view which had been rather commonly held (namely, that charisms are extraordinary signs of holiness), undoubtedly returns to a more authentic tradition that is solidly based in scripture. In this case, it returns to the genuine teaching of St. Paul, who is surely the primary source of our understanding of the charismatic gifts. The fact that this notion of charism prevailed at the Council over the one defended by Cardinal Ruffini can be seen as another fruit of the renascence of Catholic biblical studies. Credit must also be given to the pre-conciliar writings of such Catholic theologians as Yves Congar[12] and Karl Rahner,[13] whose approach to the question of charisms I found so helpful in preparing my lecture to the American bishops back in the fall of 1963.

Since the close of the Council, as one might have expected, there has been a proliferation of books and articles having to do with the charismatic element in the life of the church. Comment and discussion of the teaching of the Council on this issue was to be expected. What no one could have expected is that what was theory in the documents of the Council has since become for many Catholics a matter of personal experience. For it was less than two years after the close of Vatican II that some young Catholics at Duquesne University in Pittsburgh had a religious experience that marked the beginning of what has come to be known as the Catholic charismatic renewal. In the little more than a decade since then, hundreds of thousands of Catholics have come to participate in prayer groups and communities associated with this renewal. For most of these Catholics, this has meant being opened up to the possibility, and very often the reality, of charismatic gifts, both as they are manifested by other people in a group, and as a matter of personal experience. What is perhaps most remarkable is that a number of the charisms which have come to be seen as ordinary by participants in this renewal are ones that the Fathers of Vatican II may well have had in mind when they spoke of some charisms as extraordinary: such, for example, as prophecy, speaking in tongues, and healings through prayer.

I am well aware of the fact that the charismatic renewal raises a great many questions in the minds of Catholics who hear of the claims which its participants make, especially their claim to experience certain charisms that have been rarely seen since New Testament times. Indeed, many aspects of this renewal have raised questions in my mind, and I am far from completely satisfied that I have found the right answers to all of them. But I have been seeking answers to these questions for about eight years now, and I know that quite a few people have found the answers that I have tentatively reached a help toward understanding what is going on in this renewal. It is in the hope that my answers may prove helpful to a larger public, both participants and observers of the charismatic renewal, that I undertake the writing of this book.

Just as I am convinced that the charismatic renewal has to be examined and judged in the light of scripture and tradition, and that light from these sources is indispensable in forming our judgment on this renewal, I am equally convinced that the modern experience of charisms in the renewal is a source of light for our better understanding of what has hitherto been obscure for us in the ancient sources, when they touch on the charismatic element in the life of the church.

It is my intention, then, to bring this reciprocal light into play: to focus the light of scripture and tradition on the charismatic renewal, and to focus the light of the modern experience of charisms in the renewal on the data of scripture and tradition. Let us begin with a study of charism in our primary source: the writings of St. Paul.

TWO

Charism in St. Paul

Paul's Use of the Word Charism

Our word "charism" anglicizes the Greek word *charisma,* which is derived from the word *charis,* meaning "grace." The suffix *-ma* added to the root word *charis* forms a word whose basic meaning is "work of grace," or "gift of grace." The notion of grace (*charis*) is a key concept in the theology of St. Paul, and it is not surprising that the derived word *charisma* is also a distinctively Pauline one. Of the seventeen occurrences of this word in the New Testament, all but one are found in the Pauline corpus (the one exception is 1 Pt 4:10).

While the word *charisma* as used by Paul always reflects the basic meaning drawn from its root word *charis,* one can distinguish three different kinds of "gifts of grace" to which Paul applies the term *charisma.*

In some instances (e.g., Rom 5:15f. and 6:23) Paul uses the word *charisma* to describe the essential grace of redemption and eternal life. (Here the RSV translates *charisma* as "free gift".)

In other instances Paul uses *charisma* to describe particular gifts of divine favor, whether given to an individual (as Paul's own deliverance from danger of death: 2 Cor 1:10), or given to a people (thus Paul speaks of the privileges of the chosen people as *charismata*: Rom 11:29).

The third and most distinctively Pauline usage of the word *charisma* is found in association with the equally Pauline notion of the Christian community as "body of Christ." Here the word appears in the plural and describes the gifts of grace which are distributed among the members of the community, with a view to the role or function which each is to have. Our modern word "charism" corresponds to this third and most distinctively Pauline use of the word. We do not use the word "charism" when we intend to speak of such gifts of grace as redemption and eternal life. But it is important for us to know that Paul did, because this reminds us of the intrinsic connection between the "charisms" and the essential *charisma* of divine life which the Father has graciously given to us in Christ. The charisms are the manifold ways in which the graciousness of God is manifested in the lives of individual Christians, especially by making them effective instruments of grace to others in the body of Christ.

What makes the charisms distinct from such essential gifts of grace as redemption and eternal life, and indeed from such gifts of grace as faith, hope, and charity, is their variety and the way they are distributed among the members of the body. While everyone in the Christian community receives the same essential gifts of grace, the charisms are distributed, so that one person receives this gift, another that, and there is no one charism that everyone needs to have or should expect to have. "Each has his own special gift [*charisma*] from God, one of one kind and one of another" (1 Cor 7:7). "Having gifts [*charismata*] that differ according to the grace given to us. . . ." (Rom 12:6). "Now there are varieties of gifts [*charismata*] but the same Spirit. . . . To one is given through the Spirit the utterance of wisdom, to another the utterance of knowledge" (1 Cor 12:4, 8).

If we look at the two passages where St. Paul develops most fully his idea of these "distributed gifts of grace" (Rom 12:3-8 and 1 Cor 12), we shall also see how closely associated in Paul's thinking these gifts are with his idea of the church as "body of Christ." In the passage in Romans 12, Paul begins with the idea of the body of Christ, and moves into the idea of the "gifts that differ according to the grace given us," while in 1 Corinthians 12 he begins with a consideration of the variety of gifts, and moves into a discussion of the church as body of Christ. But the connection between these two ideas is the same in both passages. For Paul one of the basic reasons why the church is like a living body is that the multiplicity and variety of members and functions which are characteristic of any living body are also found in the church.

Where do the charisms fit into this picture? For Paul the charisms are the principle of differentiation in the body of Christ. It is the charisms that determine which function each member of the body is to have, and that enable each member to perform that function. Thus for Paul the charisms are essential to the very structure of the Christian community. In the certainly authentic letters of Paul[1] we find no other principle of differentiation in the Christian community than the charisms: no other basis for the decision as to who is to be a leader, who a teacher, who an administrator, than the charism that each one has received. There is no doubt that for Paul a Christian community without a variety of charisms operative in its members would be unthinkable; it would no longer be like a living body, and hence no longer a "body of Christ."

If the charisms are so essential to the Pauline concept of the body of Christ, one might ask why it is that, until fairly recently, Catholic theology, which surely has had much to say about the "Mystical Body," has paid so little attention to the charisms. One reason for this is that for a long time membership in the "Mystical Body" was seen almost exclusively in terms of sharing in the life of Christ by sanctifying grace. This gave rise to a tendency to conceive of the "Mystical Body" as the communion of all who actually live in Christ, whether formally members of the visible church or not. The "Mystical Body" was thought of as a kind of "sphere of grace," embracing all who were on the way to salvation. In this theory of the "Mystical Body" all attention was on sanctifying grace; hardly any attention was paid to the charisms.

For St. Paul, on the other hand, the body of Christ (which he never called "mystical") is a visible, structured community, with a variety of members with different functions, such as apostles, prophets, teachers, and the like. It is the body into which we are baptized, and in which we are made one by the

Eucharist. In this concrete, visible body of Christ the charisms are essential elements, because they determine which function each member of the body is to have. Without the charisms, one could no longer speak of the Christian community as a body, because it would lack a principle of differentiation, essential to every living body. Rediscovery of the authentic Pauline notion of the body of Christ has led inevitably to the rediscovery of the authentic Pauline notion of the charisms.

Charisms and "Spiritual Gifts" (Pneumatika)

These two terms have often been taken as synonymous, but several recent studies have suggested that there is an important distinction to be made between them. Let us look at Paul's use of these terms in 1 Corinthians 12-14.

The way that Paul introduces the question of the "spiritual gifts" in the opening phrase of 1 Corinthians 12 indicates that it was the Corinthians themselves who had raised this question. From the beginning of chapter 7, Paul is giving his solutions to problems which the Corinthians had raised in a letter which they had sent to him. See the opening words of chapter 7, "Now concerning the matters about which you wrote . . . ," and the four introductory phrases all beginning "Now concerning . . . ," which we find at 7:25, 8:1, 12:1, and 16:1. If we ask: what specifically was the nature of the problem that these gifts were causing at Corinth, there is general agreement that the answer is to be found in chapter 14. It had to do with an exaggerated esteem for the gift of tongues and an inconsiderate and unedifying use of this gift in community worship. While those who possessed this gift were using it in a way that was not building up the community, it seems likely that there were others who wanted speaking in tongues, at least in public, to be forbidden (cf. 14:39—"and do not forbid speaking in tongues"). Paul gives his detailed solution to this problem in chapter 14, but, as he so often does, before getting down to practical directives, he first lays a broad and solid doctrinal foundation for the regulations he will give. This foundation is given in chapters 12 and 13.

The question the Corinthians had raised concerned the *pneumatika* (in most English versions translated as "spiritual gifts"). From chapter 14 it is clear that in a discussion of the *pneumatika*, at least with the Corinthians, the primary examples would be tongues and prophecy. Indeed, there is no doubt that in the eyes of the Corinthians, the gift of tongues was the very highest example of the *pneumatika*. The reason for this is most likely to be found in the fact that, as we know from Paul's own usage in chapter 14, the tongue-speaker was thought to be speaking *pneumati*, that is, by the Spirit, or in the Spirit. Undoubtedly they recognized that the prophet also spoke *pneumati*, and hence would recognize both of these gifts, prophecy and tongues, as examples of *pneumatika*. How best translate this word? I suggest that rather than just "spiritual gifts," the closest English equivalent would be "gifts of inspiration." The man who speaks *pneumati* is speaking under inspiration (whether in prophecy or tongues), and that is why these are the gifts that the Corinthians thought of as the primary examples of the *pneumatika*.

If one understands the opening phrase of chapter 12 as meaning "Now concerning gifts of inspiration . . . ," it becomes easier to follow Paul's argument in the following verses. I would paraphrase the sense of verses 2 and 3 this way: "The first thing I want to remind you concerning these gifts of inspiration is that there is more than one spirit by which a person can be 'inspired.' You know how you used to be 'inspired' in your pagan rites. A man who says, 'Jesus be cursed,' may be speaking 'under inspiration,' but it will not be the Spirit of God that inspires him. Similarly, no matter how uninspired a person might seem to be who simply says, 'Jesus is Lord,' he really is speaking by the Holy Spirit."

It is very significant that while the term used in the question raised by the Corinthians' letter was *pneumatika*, Paul does not use this word again until he comes down to his specific answer to their question, at the beginning of chapter 14. In verses 4-6 of chapter 12 he uses three different words: *charismata* (gifts of grace), *diakoniai* (services), and *energemata* (workings), and of these he clearly prefers *charismata*, which he continues to use throughout chapter 12 (vv. 9, 28, 29, 31).

I have already given my reasons for thinking that, at least in the view of the Corinthians, the *pneumatika* were those activities in which a person was most obviously speaking or acting *pneumati,* that is, under inspiration. They evidently saw glossolalia as the strongest evidence that a person was speaking under inspiration, and hence esteemed tongue-speaking as the highest of the *pneumatika.*

To my mind, Paul's treatment of the *charismata* in chapter 12 is intended to show that it is a mistake to limit the Spirit's activity in the community to such "gifts of inspiration." Paul certainly includes the gifts of tongues and prophecy among the *charismata.* But he insists that there are many other gifts of grace (*charismata*), many services (*diakoniai*), and many workings of God (*energemata*), which are likewise "manifestations of the Spirit." And, above all, he insists that the criterion by which the excellence of the Spirit's gifts is to be measured is not the degree of "inspiration," but the degree to which they contribute to the building-up of the community. It is the very nature of all these gifts that they are "manifestations of the Spirit *for a useful purpose*" (*pros to sumpheron*: 12:7).

As I see it, the critique implied in Paul's preference for the term *charismata* over the Corinthians' word *pneumatika* can be expressed this way: "You Corinthians seem to think that the only real gifts of the Spirit are ones that can be called 'gifts of inspiration.' Well, your notion of the Spirit's working in the church is far too narrow. There are many other gifts and services that are equally 'manifestations of the Spirit,' even though they do not seem to involve any special inspiration, and you might not think of them as *pneumatika.*" Indeed, there is reason to wonder whether the Corinthians would have thought of such prosaic services as "helping" and "administrating" as *pneumatika,* whereas for Paul they were certainly among the *charismata* (12:28). In fact, there is little doubt that in Paul's mind, *all* of these gifts, as "manifestations of the Spirit," could rightly be called "*pneumatika,*" since "it is one and the same Spirit who works them all" (12:11). What I believe Paul is criticizing here is the Corinthians' tendency to see the Spirit's working primarily, if not exclusively, in such "gifts of inspiration" as tongues and prophecy. I believe that his use of the term *pneumatika* here reflects both the way the Corinthians were using this term, and his own critique of their use of it.

This interpretation seems to me to be confirmed by Paul's treatment of the Corinthians' claim to be *pneumatikoi*: "spiritual men."

"Spiritual Men" (Pneumatikoi)

The fact that the Corinthians—or at least a significant number of them—were claiming to be *pneumatikoi*, is implied in Paul's rebuke in 1 Corinthians 3:1: "But I, brethren, could not address you as spiritual men [*pneumatikoi*], but as men of the flesh." This leads us to ask on what grounds the Corinthians based their claim to be *pneumatikoi*. I suggest that the answer to this question is to be found at 14:37, where Paul says, "If anyone thinks that he is a prophet, or *pneumatikos*, he should acknowledge that what I am writing to you is a command of the Lord." At the end of this chapter, a chapter in which the whole argument turned on the relative merits of prophecy and tongues, there can be little doubt that the basis of the Corinthians' claim to be *pneumatikoi* was their possession of these "gifts of inspiration," the *pneumatika*. The usual translation of 14:37, "If anyone thinks that he is a prophet or spiritual," hardly brings out the real meaning here; I suggest translating, "If anyone thinks that he is a prophet or charismatic."

Indeed, Paul does not deny that the Corinthians are "charismatic"; what he does deny is that this, in itself, guarantees that they are truly "spiritual men." This distinction between the two senses of the word *pneumatikoi* ("charismatic" for the Corinthians; "spiritual" for Paul) lies at the heart of the whole argument of 1 Corinthians. The burden of Paul's message is this: having an abundance of the gifts of the Spirit is no guarantee of truly living by the Spirit; it is only those who live by the Spirit who are truly "spiritual men." Let us see how Paul develops this argument in the earlier part of this letter.

In his opening prayer Paul thanked God and congratulated the Corinthians for the way God had enriched them with charisms, mentioning in particular the gifts of speech and knowledge (1:5). The burden of Paul's argument from 1:18 through chapter 3 suggests that they prided themselves on their wisdom. The rebuke in 3:1-4 makes it clear that they also considered themselves to be *pneumatikoi*.

It is instructive to see how Paul handles each of these claims. He does not deny that they have gifts of wisdom and knowledge, or that they possess *pneumatika*, the "spiritual gifts" on which they evidently based their claim to be *pneumatikoi*: "spiritual people." But in each case we see how Paul sets out to correct their defective view of what true wisdom and knowledge are, and what it means to be a truly spiritual person.

In chapters 1-3 Paul draws a sharp contrast between human wisdom and the true wisdom which is folly in the eyes of men, but is in fact the wisdom of God. This true wisdom is none other than the wisdom of the cross. The whole argument here suggests strongly that the Corinthians were missing this essential point about genuine Christian wisdom. Similarly the argument of chapter 8 shows how imperfect the Corinthians' knowledge was. It was a kind of knowledge that "puffed up," because it was not governed by love in its application to concrete practice, where following one's superior knowledge could work spiritual harm to a less enlightened Christian. Finally, the argument of 3:1-4 shows how weak in Paul's eyes was the Corinthians' claim to be "spiritual men." For Paul the genuinely spiritual person is one who has the "mind of Christ" (2:16). He does not further spell out here what is positively required, but he does mention negative qualities that prove that the Corinthians, no matter how "charismatic" they are, are still not really "spiritual." For, after congratulating them that there is no charism that they lack, Paul goes on to say, "But I, brethren, could not address you as spiritual men, but as men of the flesh. . . . For while there is jealousy and strife among you, are you not of the flesh, and behaving like ordinary men?" (3:1, 3). Later on, in chapter 13, we see that it is love that excludes all such "unspiritual" attitudes as jealousy (cf. 13:4); from this, one may safely conclude that for Paul the truly spiritual person will be distinguished by love.

This interpretation of Paul's criteria for judging someone to be truly spiritual is confirmed by his teaching in the Letter to the Galatians. Here the spiritual person is the one who "walks by the Spirit" (5:16), who "is led by the Spirit" (5:18), and who "lives by the Spirit" (5:25). Such are the "spiritual men" who can "restore in a spirit of gentleness a man who is overtaken in a trespass" (6:1). How are such "spiritual men" to be known? While Paul does not quote the saying, "By their fruits you shall know them," there is no doubt that this is the criterion which he applies, for he describes both the "works of the flesh" and the "fruit of the Spirit" (5:19-23). If one compares the qualities which Paul lists as the "fruit of the Spirit" with his description of love in 1 Corinthians 13, it is obvious that "walking in the Spirit" is the same as "walking in love." The truly spiritual person is the one who keeps the "one word in which the whole law is fulfilled: 'You shall love your neighbor as yourself'" (5:14).

On the other hand, if there is one thing that is clear from 1 Corinthians 13, it is that the possession of charismatic gifts is no guarantee that their possessor is "walking in love." For Paul it is evidently not at all impossible that a person could have tongues, prophecy, knowledge, and the rest, and still lack the basic virtue of love. In other words, a person could be highly "charismatic," and yet not be a truly "spiritual" person. Here again we see the ambiguity of the Corinthians' claim to be "spiritual men" on the basis of their "spiritual gifts."

Given the confusion that has often surrounded the notions "charism" and "charismatic," it is important to know what sort of things St. Paul himself thought of as typical charisms. In the next chapter we shall look at the various lists of charisms that we find in his letters.

THREE

Notes on the Pauline Charisms

The Lists of Charisms in 1 Corinthians 12

The list of nine charisms which we find in 1 Corinthians 12:8-10 has often been treated as if it were *the* list of Pauline charisms, if not a complete list, at least as some sort of an ideal list. The arguments against taking it this way seem to me to be altogether convincing. First of all, in this very same chapter in verse 28, Paul gives us another list, in which some of the gifts mentioned in verses 8-10 do not appear, while others are added. Second, in his letter to the Romans (12:6-8), Paul gives quite a different list of charisms, even though his teaching about the gifts and their role in the body of Christ is substantially the same as we have it, more fully developed, in 1 Corinthians 12.

How explain the difference between the lists in Romans 12 and Corinthians 12? The most likely explanation lies in the fact that while Paul knew the Corinthian community at first hand, he had not yet visited Rome when he wrote to that church. There are very good reasons for judging that the list of charisms in 1 Corinthians 12:8-10 reflects Paul's personal knowledge of the particular gifts most in evidence among the Corinthians at that time. We have seen how Paul began his letter by congratulating the Corinthians on their rich gifts of speech (*logos*) and knowledge (*gnosis*). We have also seen how he then proceeded to criticize their kind of wisdom (*sophia*), and the way they were using their knowledge to the harm of their neighbors' conscience. Hence it is no surprise that the first two gifts mentioned in his list of charisms here are *logos sophias* (utterance of wisdom) and *logos gnoseos* (utterance of knowledge). Nor, in the light of chapter 14, which treats at length of the gifts of prophecy, tongues, and interpretation of tongues, is it any surprise that these gifts also appear in this list. The fact that the gifts of tongues and interpretation come in the last place each time that Paul enumerates the gifts in chapter 12 (vv. 10, 28, 30) is surely no accident, in view of his intention in chapter 14 to moderate the Corinthians' excessive esteem for speaking in tongues. Nor is it any surprise that in chapter 13 the gifts that Paul insists are going to pass away are prophecy, tongues, and knowledge—without doubt the three gifts on which the Corinthians most prided themselves.

On the other hand, given the fact that Paul had no personal acquaintance with the community at Rome when he wrote to that church, it is logical to surmise that the charisms which Paul mentions in Romans 12:6-8 are such as he would expect to find in any Christian community. In view of this, it is significant that prophecy appears in this list, and indeed in the first place, but there is no mention of such gifts as healings, miracles, tongues, or interpretation of tongues. Can it be that while Paul would have expected to find the gift of prophecy in any Christian community, he was not so sure that these other gifts were in evidence at Rome?

In any case, the evidence seems convincing that Paul's choice of the nine charisms which he lists in 1 Corinthians 12:8-10 was determined by the actual situation at Corinth, and to a considerable extent by the problems which some of these gifts were raising in that community. There is, then, no sound reason for taking these particular nine gifts to be *the* charisms in any privileged sense. It is even more obvious that they cannot be taken to be *the* charisms in an exclusive sense, since Paul mentions others both at the end of this same chapter (12:28) and in Romans 12. Indeed, there is good reason to doubt whether it is possible to draw up an exhaustive list of all the charisms. This would suppose that all possible charisms are already mentioned in the New Testament. But this would mean that the Holy Spirit would be limited to giving only those gifts which he had already given to the church in apostolic times. Surely the living Spirit, who guides the church throughout the course of history, has given and will continue to give new gifts to meet new needs of the church in every age, with sovereign freedom as Lord of his gifts.

At the same time, it is instructive for us to know what kind of things the New Testament writers recognized as charisms. In the following pages I shall offer some notes and observations on the charisms mentioned by St. Paul. Let us first look more closely at what we find in 1 Corinthians 12:4-10.

Now there are varieties of gifts, but the same Spirit; and there are varieties of service, but the same Lord; and there are varieties of working, but it is the same God who inspires them all in every one.
(12:4-6)

The word translated "varieties" in the Revised Standard Version can also mean "distributions," and it is probable that Paul has both meanings in mind here. It is typical of the charisms that they are distributed graces. Paul uses three terms: *charismata* (gifts), *diakoniai* (services), and *energemata* (workings), and seems to attribute the charisms to the Spirit, the services to the Lord Jesus, and the workings to God the Father. However, the fact that elsewhere he can attribute all these gifts to the Spirit (12:11), or to God (12:28), shows that the trinitarian formula is simply a way of stressing the divine origin of all these gifts. Likewise there is general agreement among commentators that the three terms used here are not intended to describe three distinct categories of gifts, but rather to stress the fact that all these grace-gifts (*charismata*) are meant for service (*diakonia*) and all are workings of divine power (*energemata*).

To each is given the manifestation of the Spirit for the common good. (12:7)

I am quoting the Revised Standard Version, but I would prefer to translate the last phrase here as "for a useful purpose." The Greek words, *pros to sumpheron,* mean: "with a view to what is profitable." The translation "for the common good" would be misleading, if it were taken to mean that a gift primarily useful to the person having it could not be classed as a charism, on the grounds that it would not be serving the common good. That this is not Paul's intention is clear from the fact that on the one hand he lists the gift of tongues among the charisms, and on the other hand he says that the one who speaks in tongues "edifies himself" (14:4). What Paul requires of a charism is that it be useful or profitable, or, to use a favorite term of Paul's, that it be upbuilding (edifying). We see a typical use of these terms in an earlier passage of this same letter: " 'All things are lawful,' but not all things are helpful [*sumpherei*]. 'All things are lawful,' but not all things build up" (10:23). So when Paul describes a charism as "a manifestation of the Spirit for a useful purpose," he is equivalently saying: "for edification." This is why his criterion for judging the relative worth of charisms is their usefulness, or the way they build people up.

How are we to understand that these gifts are "manifestations of the Spirit"? It seems most likely that what Paul has in mind is the way that the exercise of these gifts reveals the presence of the Spirit, without whose influence the person could not speak or act as he does. We can compare what St. Peter said at Pentecost about the outpouring of the Spirit: "Having received from the Father the promise of the Spirit, he has poured out this which you see and hear" (Acts 2:33). What the risen Christ has "poured out" is the Holy Spirit, and it is as though the Spirit himself is being "seen and heard" in the Pentecostal gifts.

Finally, we note that Paul says, "To each is given." Does that mean that each and every Christian receives some charism? This may well have been Paul's own experience, and his expectation as well, but in itself the expression "to each" stresses more the idea of distribution than the idea of universality.

To one is given through the Spirit the utterance of wisdom, and to another the utterance of knowledge according to the same Spirit.
(12:8)

The first point to be noticed here is that Paul does not speak simply of wisdom and knowledge as charisms, but in both cases it is the *logos,* the word or utterance, that he mentions as the charism. As we have already seen, Paul speaks of the Corinthians as being "enriched . . . with all speech and all knowledge" (1:5), and then goes on to criticize their kind of wisdom, and the way they were making use of their superior knowledge. Perhaps his limitation of the charism to the "utterance" of wisdom or knowledge is intended to bring out the idea that it is only by the actual utterance that a person's wisdom or knowledge can be judged to be a real gift of the Spirit.

What is the difference between a "word of wisdom" and a "word of knowledge"? In Paul's vocabulary the terms are not always clearly distinguished, and some commentators say there is no consistent difference between them in Pauline usage. But if we look at the way Paul has used these terms in 1 Corinthians, we see that he has given us an example of a "word of knowledge" in 8:4—'An idol has no real existence.' If we judge by this example, we could say that a word of knowledge is an insight into reality. In the example given, this is not merely theoretical knowledge, but is the basis for a practical decision: "Therefore one may eat meat sacrificed to idols."

Paul's treatment of wisdom is more complex, because he distinguishes between "wisdom of men" (1 Cor 2:5, 13) and "the wisdom of God" (2:7). The latter is the wisdom hidden from the rulers of this world, which God has revealed to us through the Spirit (2:7-10). This wisdom is identified with the person of Christ: "Christ Jesus, whom God made our wisdom" (1:30). It would seem then that for Paul "wisdom" retains much of its Old Testament connotation of an appreciative grasp of God's plan of salvation. A "word of wisdom," then, would most likely be an utterance manifesting some new insight into the mystery of redemption through Christ. The letters of Paul offer us numerous examples of such "words of wisdom," in the form of Paul's insights into the plan of salvation for the Gentiles.

To another faith by the same Spirit (12:9)

The kind of faith that belongs in a list of distributed charisms is not the faith by which "the just man lives" (Rom 1:17), and without which it is impossible to please God. Rather, it is the kind of faith that can "move mountains" (1 Cor 13:2), in other words, a gift of confidence in God's intention to intervene powerfully in a particular situation. Such was the faith with which Peter said to the lame man at the gate of the temple: "In the name of Jesus Christ of Nazareth, walk" (Acts 3:6).

To another gifts of healing by the one Spirit (12:9)

This is the Revised Standard Version translation; literally the Greek means "charisms of healings," where both substantives are plural. Paul speaks of this gift three times in this chapter (vv. 9, 28, 30), and each time he uses the same formula. Hence it is to be noted that Paul does not speak of anyone as having "the gift of healing" (which would suggest a habitual power to heal people), but he sees each healing as a distinct charism, or gift of grace. The fact that "charisms of healings" are given to one person suggests that certain people are used with some frequency as channels or instruments of the divine power to heal. But there is nothing here to justify speaking of a "gift of healing," understood as a habitual charismatic power to heal the sick, nor is there any textual basis for the Revised Standard

Version translation, "healers," in verse 28. Here also the Greek means "charisms of healings."

To another the working of miracles (12:10)

Here again the Revised Standard Version is misleading, as it suggests that someone's charism is the "working of miracles." But, as is the case with healings, Paul uses two nouns in the plural: *energemata dunameon.* We have seen the word *energemata* above in verse 6, where we learned that while there are varieties of "workings," it is God who works all these things in everyone. The other noun here, which literally means "power," is used in the New Testament also in the concrete sense of "deeds of power," such as miracles and exorcisms. An example of this usage is Acts 19:11-12, where both miracles and exorcisms are described as the *dunameis,* or "deeds of power," which God worked through the hands of Paul. So the two words, *energemata dunameon,* literally mean "workings of deeds of power." The use of the two plural nouns emphasizes Paul's idea that each miracle or other manifestation of divine power is a distinct charism. If many such charisms are given to one individual, it is because God chooses to use that person with some frequency as an instrument of his "works of power," as we know that he used Peter and Paul.

To another prophecy (12:10)
(I shall postpone detailed study of this gift to chapter 7.)

To another the ability to distinguish between spirits (12:10)

In the literature of Pentecostalism and the charismatic renewal, this gift has often been understood as the ability to detect the presence and influence of evil spirits. But I agree with the consensus of New Testament scholars that the gift which Paul had in mind here is primarily concerned with the one preceding it in the list, namely, prophecy. Prophecy is "inspired speech," and the discernment of spirits has to do with determining by what spirit the speaker is "inspired." As we have seen above, for Paul, "spirit" and "inspiration" are ambivalent terms. The grace of discerning spirits is the grace-given ability to see beneath the phenomenon of inspiration and to judge correctly whether the speaker is really being inspired by the Holy Spirit or not.

To another various kinds of tongues, to another the interpretation of tongues (12:10)

(I shall discuss these gifts below, in chapter 8.)
We now move on to the end of 1 Corinthians 12, where Paul gives us another list of gifts.

And God has appointed in the church (12:28)

This is to be seen as the counterpoint to verse 18: "But as it is, God arranged the organs in the body, each one of them, as he chose." As it is God who gave the various organs to our physical body, so it is God who distributes the various gifts to the members of the body of Christ.

First apostles, second prophets, third teachers (12:28)

This is the only time that Paul explicitly indicates an order among the gifts. In this list, after the first three, Paul does not continue a numbered sequence for the rest, but it is to be noted that the gift of tongues is put in the last place. It is also noteworthy that the first three terms in this list—and they alone—are words that describe the persons having the gifts, rather than the gifts themselves. Thus, strictly speaking, the charism is prophecy (cf. 12:10), but here Paul speaks of "prophets." All three words—apostles, prophets, teachers— refer to persons having clearly defined roles and recognized ministries in the community.

It hardly needs to be said that in Paul's vocabulary the term "apostle" is not limited to the "twelve." For example, among the witnesses to the risen Christ, whom Paul lists in 1 Corinthians 15:5-9, "all the apostles" of verse 7 are surely not to be identified in an exclusive sense with "the twelve" of verse 5. And of course Paul confidently asserts his own claim to be an apostle even if "the least of the apostles" (v. 9).

"Prophets" are evidently important members of the church in Paul's eyes. Along with the apostles, they are the receivers of revelation (Eph 3:5), and it is on "the foundation of the apostles and prophets" that the church is built (Eph 2:20). It hardly seems likely that Paul would number among the "prophets" every man or woman who might occasionally receive an inspiration to prophesy (cf. 1 Cor 11:4-5). Hence it seems necessary to distinguish between the recognized ministry of the prophet and the occasional gift of prophecy. We leave further discussion of this gift to chapter 7.

"Teachers" also have a stable ministry in the community. We find them also in the churches of Rome (Rom 12:7) and Antioch (Acts 13:1). On the other hand, in 1 Corinthians 14:26 it seems possible that someone who is not a recognized teacher might receive an occasional charism of teaching (the word translated as "lesson" in the Revised Standard Version is *didache,* teaching).

Apostles, prophets, and teachers appear again among the "gifts of Christ to the church" which are named in Ephesians 4:11. The word "charism" does not appear in that text, but the idea is virtually expressed in verse 7: "Grace was given to each of us according to the measure of Christ's gift." Here it is the risen Christ who "gave apostles, prophets, evangelists, pastors and teachers" for the building up of his body.

Then workers of miracles, then healers (12:28)

This translation is misleading because it suggests that, as there are recognized apostles, prophets, and teachers in the church, so there are people with a recognized ministry of working miracles or healing the sick. But this is not what Paul's text says. After the first three terms, which do refer to the persons having stable ministries in the church, Paul reverts to terms he has already used in his previous list of charisms: namely, *dunameis* (deeds of power) and *charismata iamaton* (charisms of healings). As we have seen above, these terms bring out Paul's view that each miracle, each healing, is a distinct charism. Paul does not speak of anyone having a "charism of working miracles" or a "charism of healing the sick." While he speaks of prophets and teachers, he does not speak of "miracle-workers" or "healers."

Helpers, administrators (12:28)

Here again, the Revised Standard Version gives us English words that refer to people having the gifts, whereas the Greek text has words that instead express the gifts themselves. Here also the words are in the plural and are difficult to translate literally. An approximation to the literal sense would be to say "acts of helping" and "acts of governing." Again Paul's use of the plural nouns brings out the idea that each of these activities is a distinct charism. It should also be noted that these are charisms which Paul did not mention in the previous list (12:8-10).

Are all apostles? Are all prophets? Are all teachers? Do all work miracles? Do all possess gifts of healing? Do all speak with tongues? (12:29-30)

These rhetorical questions, obviously expecting the answer no, show that there is no one charism which all should expect to have. Significantly, this includes the gift of tongues. In some literature of the charismatic renewal the impression is given that everyone should expect to receive the gift of tongues, frequently on the basis of 1 Corinthians 14:5, where Paul says, "Now, I want you all to speak in tongues." But this wish on Paul's part is expressed in exactly the same way as his wish in 1 Corinthians 7:7 that all might have the gift of celibacy: "I wish that all were as I myself am." The Greek word translated "I want" or "I wish" is the same in both places, and in both contexts would be better translated "I should like it if." Such a wish expresses Paul's esteem for these gifts, but in neither case does it imply a judgment on his part that everyone should have or should expect to receive these gifts.

But earnestly desire the higher gifts (12:31a).

The word translated "gifts" here is Paul's preferred term, *charismata,* and the word translated "earnestly desire" is *zeloute,* which grammatically could be taken either as indicative or as imperative. Some commentators who take it as indicative ("You are earnestly seeking the higher gifts") understand that Paul is rebuking the Corinthians for not remaining satisfied with the gift that each one has received, and for ambitioning higher ones.[1]

However, if we look forward to the first verse of chapter 14, we find the same verb *zeloute* in a context where there is no doubt about its being in the imperative: "Earnestly desire the spiritual gifts [*pneumatika*], especially that you may prophesy." Why would Paul rebuke the Corinthians for seeking the "better charisms" in chapter 12, when he is going to encourage them to seek the "spiritual gifts," and indeed the better one (prophecy) in chapter 14? One answer that has been given to this question involves a theory about the difference between the *charismata* and the *pneumatika.* According to this theory, the *charismata* are the gifts by which God assigns each person's place and function in the body. Therefore we must simply accept the charism which God assigns us, and it would be sinful ambition to seek the "better charisms." On the other hand, again according to this theory, the *pneumatika* are transitory, occasional gifts, which do not involve an assigned status in the body, and which therefore it is legitimate to seek.[2]

Now such a theory might stand up if Paul had restricted his use of the term *charisma* to such clearly defined functions in the church as "apostles, prophets, and teachers," and had described all the transitory, occasional gifts as *pneumatika*. But he did not do so. The gifts of prophecy and tongues, which he calls *pneumatika* in chapter 14, are also included among the *charismata* in chapter 12, with no trace of a distinction between the stable function of the prophet as a *charisma*, and the occasional gift of prophecy as one of the *pneumatika*, or between a recognized charism of being a tongue-speaker and the occasional spiritual gift of tongues.

I have explained above my reasons for thinking that the term *pneumatika* was being used at Corinth to describe the "gifts of inspiration," and that Paul wanted the Corinthians to recognize a much broader spectrum of "manifestations of the Spirit," which he called "charisms, services and workings." Given the fact that in 14:1 Paul encourages the Corinthians to seek the *pneumatika*, I find it impossible to think that in 12:31 he would have intended to rebuke them for seeking the better *charismata*. What he intended to correct was their faulty judgment as to which were the better gifts, and the unsound criterion on which their judgment was based.

And I will show you a still more excellent way (12:31b).

It is sometimes said that love is the highest of the charisms, and that, having love, one has no need of any other charism. Such a view cannot be based on Paul's teaching. Paul does not put love into a list of charisms (even at the top of the list), because it does not belong in the same category with the charisms. These are distributed gifts: one has this, another has that, and there is no one charism that everyone has to have. But everyone has to have love; without this fundamental gift of grace, no charism is of any value, as Paul goes on to say in chapter 13. At the end of chapter 12 he does not say, "I will now tell you which is the best of the charisms"; he speaks of a "more excellent way." This expression could be better translated: "a way that is beyond compare"; the Greek has the force not merely of a comparative but of a superlative.

What is not always clearly understood is that love is the

motive for seeking the "better charisms." This follows from the fact that the better charisms are those which are more useful for building up the community.

Charisms and Love (1 Cor 13)

It is not my intention to offer a detailed exegesis of Paul's famous chapter on love, but to see what further light this chapter throws on Paul's teaching on the charisms. Let us first look at verses one to three.

If I speak in the tongues of men and of angels, but have not love, I am a noisy gong or a clanging cymbal. And if I have prophetic powers, and understand all mysteries and all knowledge, and if I have all faith, so as to remove mountains, but have not love, I am nothing. If I give away all I have, and if I deliver my body to be burned, but have not love, I gain nothing.

In these three verses we find a new listing of charisms: tongues, prophecy, understanding of mysteries, knowledge, faith, giving away all one's possessions, and giving oneself up to death. Paul clearly intends to arrange these gifts in an ascending order, building up to a climax. The mention therefore of tongues in the first place here is consistent with his intention to moderate the Corinthians' excessive esteem for this gift. The expression "tongues of men and of angels" is most likely to be taken as equivalent to "the most marvellous tongues imaginable." There is no proof that Paul really identified charismatic tongues with the languages of angels.

And if I have prophetic powers

The Greek word translated "prophetic powers" in the Revised Standard Version is simply the word "prophecy," which we have seen already mentioned in Paul's first list in 12:10.

And understand all mysteries and all knowledge

The repeated word "all" shows that Paul is not talking about an ordinary gift of knowledge, but the greatest possible gift. It is worth noting that Paul links "knowledge of mysteries" with prophetic gifts also in Ephesians 3:4-5, where he speaks of his own "insight into the mystery of Christ," a mystery which has only "now been revealed to his holy apostles and prophets by the Spirit."

And if I have all faith, so as to remove mountains

This is the verse which explains how the charism of faith, mentioned in 12:9, is to be understood. Evidently Paul knew this saying of Jesus (cf. Mt 17:20).

If I give away all I have

This would be the highest exercise of the charism mentioned in Romans 12:8: "He who contributes [better: shares his goods], in liberality."

And if I deliver my body to be burned

There is no doubt that it is a question of giving oneself up to death, but there is some textual support for reading the last phrase as meaning: "in order that I may boast." If this is the correct reading, it can be taken as another way of saying "without love."

I am nothing. . . . I gain nothing.

Note that it is the person having the charism who is worth nothing and gains nothing if he lacks love. Paul does not say that a lack of love on the part of the person having a charism necessarily means that the charism itself loses all its value or effectiveness for other people, who may profit from its exercise, even when the person having the charism does not. It is also clear from this whole development that Paul accepts as a realistic possibility that a person could have even great charismatic gifts and lack the virtue of love. In this same letter, Paul both congratulated the Corinthians that they lacked no charism, and castigated them for their lack of love, which manifested itself in their jealousies, party strife, inconsiderate use of their superior knowledge, and even gross selfishness at the "Lord's supper." He did not deny that they had an abundance of "spiritual gifts," but he did not agree that this was enough to qualify them as truly "spiritual people."

Love never ends; as for prophecies, they will pass away; as for tongues, they will cease; as for knowledge, it will pass away. For our knowledge is imperfect and our prophecy is imperfect; but when the perfect comes, the imperfect will pass away.

(13:8-10)

The three gifts which Paul says are going to pass away are without doubt the three which the Corinthians held in highest esteem. We also know that two of them, knowledge and tongues, were the source of problems which Paul set out to correct in this letter (see chapter 8 on knowledge and chapter 14 on tongues).

What does Paul mean when he says that these gifts are going to pass away? Interpreters who follow what is called the theory of "dispensationalism" take Paul to mean that these gifts were intended only for the earliest period of the church's history. Accordingly, they refuse to recognize any genuine charism of prophecy or tongues in the post-apostolic era. But modern biblical scholars agree that the time when the "perfect" will come and "we shall see face to face" refers not to any point in the ongoing history of the church, but to the future age. Hence it is only at the close of this age that Paul expects the charisms to cease, whereas love will continue in the world to come.

Charisms in Romans 12

Since I shall give a detailed treatment of 1 Corinthians 14 later on in discussing prophecy and tongues, let us move now to look at what Paul says about the charisms in Romans 12:3-8.

> *For by the grace given to me I bid every one among you not to think of himself more highly than he ought to think, but to think with sober judgment, each according to the measure of faith which God has assigned him* (v. 3).

Of what kind of faith is Paul speaking here? I believe that James D.G. Dunn is correct in his view that this is not the faith by which "the just man lives," but a charismatic faith, of which God assigns a different measure to different people. Such faith, as Dunn puts it, is an "assurance that God is speaking or acting through the charismatic's words or actions."[3] The "assigned measure of faith," in this sense, will be a gift concomitant and proportionate to each of the charisms. It is the assurance that allows a person to "step out in faith" to exercise the charism that he or she has received.

> *For as in one body we have many members, and all the members do not have the same function, so we, though many, are one body in Christ, and individually members one of another. Having gifts that differ according to the grace given to us. . . .* (vv. 4-6a)

It is important to see the connection in Paul's thought between our being "one body in Christ" and our "having gifts that differ." The connecting link is the fact that a living body is made up of many members having different functions. The key words are *praxis* (function) and *charismata* (gifts). The fact that we have "gifts that differ according to the grace given to us" means that each of us has a particular function in the community, and it is for that reason that we are like organs of a living body, each having its own function, and all contributing to the well-being of the whole body.

Let us use them (v. 6a)

This phrase which the Revised Standard Version introduces at this point suggests that in the following verses, Paul is giving an exhortation as to how each of the charisms is to be exercised, e.g., "with liberality, with zeal, with cheerfulness." But there is nothing in the Greek text that corresponds to the words "let us use them." Having said that we have "gifts that differ according to the grace given to us," it would seem that in each case Paul names the gift, along with the grace that is proper to each of the gifts. Thus, charismatic sharing of goods will be characterized by liberality, charismatic acts of mercy by cheerfulness, etc.

If prophecy, in proportion to our faith (v. 6b)

I take this to mean that the grace proper to the gift of prophecy is to prophesy only to the extent that one receives the grace of assurance that the word one is going to speak is really a word from the Lord to those who are going to hear it. "Faith" in this context is assurance or confidence that one is receiving a genuine inspiration to speak. Of course such confidence has to be tested in the light of subsequent discernment by the community of the prophecy that has been spoken.

If service, in our serving (v. 7a)

Whereas in 1 Corinthians 12:5 Paul had used the term "varieties of services" as a generic description of charismatic gifts, he now speaks of a "charism of service," evidently having something more specific in mind. One example of what Paul no doubt recognized as such a "charism of service" is found in 1 Corinthians 16:15-16, where Paul says: "Now, brethren, you know that the household of Stephanas were the first converts in Achaia, and they have devoted themselves to the service of the saints; I urge you to be subject to such men and to every fellow worker and laborer." From Paul's exhortation to "be subject to such men," we can surmise that the service which Stephanas and others like him were rendering involved some kind of a leadership role in the community.

He who teaches, in his teaching (v. 7b)

We have seen that on the one occasion when Paul numbered the charisms in the order of their importance, the third in the list, after apostles and prophets, were the teachers (1 Cor 12:28). We have also remarked that since Paul had never visited Rome when he wrote to that church, it is logical to assume that the charisms which he lists in Romans 12 are ones that he would expect to be operative in any Christian community. In view of this, it is significant that both prophecy and teaching are included in this list. Evidently Paul saw both of these as essential to the life of the local church. Apostles, on the other hand, had a primary role as founders of churches, but Paul would not expect each local church to have its "resident apostle."

He who exhorts, in his exhortation (v. 8a)

This suggests that Paul expected that in a Christian community there would be someone with a particular gift for exhortation. In 1 Corinthians 14:3 the same word here translated "exhortation" (*paraklesis*) is used to describe one of the functions of a prophet: "He who prophesies speaks to men for their upbuilding, and encouragement [*paraklesis*], and consolation." It would seem that while a prophet's message might be a word of exhortation, another person might have a special gift for exhortation without also having the gift of prophecy.

He who contributes, in liberality (v. 8b)

We know from Paul's instructions concerning the collection for the church in Jerusalem that he expected everyone to contribute to this according to his means: "Now concerning the contribution for the saints: as I directed the churches of Galatia, so you also are to do. On the first day of every week, each of you is to put something aside and store it up, as he may prosper, so that contributions need not be made when I come" (1 Cor 16:1-2). When we find "contributing," or more accurately, "sharing one's goods," listed as one of the charisms, we must conclude that here Paul has in mind an outstanding gift of liberality in sharing one's goods with others.

He who gives aid, with zeal (v. 8c)

The word which the Revised Standard Version translates here as "he who gives aid" can also mean "he who rules"; at 1 Thessalonians 5:12 the Revised Standard Version translates the same word as "those who are over you." At Romans 12:8 the New English Bible has "leader," and the New American Bible has "he who rules." Accepting this as the preferable translation, we can see this gift as corresponding to the "acts of governing" which Paul mentioned in 1 Corinthians 12:28. We have also seen how Paul urged the Corinthians to "be subject to" Stephanas and the others who had put themselves at the service of the community.

He who does acts of mercy, with cheerfulness. (v. 8d)

Just as the charism of "contributing" includes the grace of doing this with liberality, so the charism of doing acts of mercy includes the grace of doing this cheerfully.

This completes our study of charisms in the writings of St. Paul. It will be recalled that the definition of charisms given by the Second Vatican Council described them as "special graces by which the Holy Spirit makes the faithful able and willing to undertake various tasks or services advantageous for the renewal and upbuilding of the Church." It is significant that of these two goals, the *renewal* of the church is mentioned in the first place. In the next chapter we are going to consider the role which charisms and charismatic movements have played in the renewal of the church throughout its history, and then we shall look at a movement which calls itself "charismatic" and is seeking the renewal of the church in our day.

FOUR

Charismatic Movements and Church Renewal

THERE ARE TWO DISTINCT, but equally important, ways that the Holy Spirit breathes life into the body of Christ: on the one hand, by his covenant relationship with the church, guaranteeing the effectiveness of its sacraments and official ministries, and on the other, by his unpredictable and often surprising charismatic interventions. For the purpose of safeguarding and handing on tradition, a system with established offices of leadership is needed. But it is equally true that for the purpose of shaking the church out of the complacency and mediocrity that inevitably creep into any institution, the church needs the charismatic interventions of the Spirit.

Human experience shows how rarely any established institution will undertake and carry through a radical reform and renewal of itself on its own initiative. History shows that in this respect the church has not differed greatly from other institutions. At the same time, history shows not only that the church has survived longer than any other comparable institution, but also that over the centuries there have been many movements by which the life of the church has been profoundly renewed. In most cases such renewal movements have shown the spontaneity and unpredictability that are typical of the charismatic. The most unlikely people have been the chosen instruments to initiate and lead such movements. For the most part they have been "grassroots" movements,

coming from "below" rather than planned from the "top."
They have usually had something of the surprising or even
somewhat shocking about them. They have frequently aroused
the initial opposition of the guardians of the established order,
and only with difficulty been accepted as movements genuinely
inspired by the Spirit.

Obviously this is not the place to attempt a detailed account
of the many charismatic movements that have profoundly
renewed the inner life of the church in the course of its history.
Suffice it to name at least a few of them, such as the ascetical
movements of the fourth and fifth centuries, the spread of
monasticism in the West with St. Benedict and his followers,
the Cluniac and Cistercian reforms, the Franciscan movement
(perhaps the most thoroughly charismatic, in its primitive
period, that the church has ever known), the various renewals of
lay spirituality during the late Middle Ages, the work of the
Jesuits and others to renew Catholic life in the post-Reformation
period, the renewal of eucharistic and liturgical life in the
present century.

I think one can say that in each of these renewal movements
there has been a realization of the saying about the "householder
who brings out of his treasure what is new and what is old" (Mt
13:52). Each of these movements has involved a going back to
what is old, i.e., a return to the basic message and challenge of
the gospel. But each of them has also involved something new
and distinctive, a new way of meeting the challenge of the
gospel, a fresh approach, more appropriate to the needs of its
times. It is this newness and freshness that characterize the
charismatic activity of the Spirit in the church.

While the movements that we have mentioned, and many
others besides, have had an important role in renewing the
church's life at various crucial times in its history, the story of
movements that set out to renew the church is not one of
uniform success. The most frequent cause of failure is that the
participants in such a movement eventually became alienated
from the church which they intended to renew. In some cases
this has meant the collapse of the movement; in others it has

been the beginning of a new church or sect. Whether the blame for such a separation falls more on the mother church or on the group that became separated from her, the fact is that such a separation frustrated the original intention of the movement to bring about a renewal of the church. I certainly do not think that the fact of separation by itself is proof that the movement in question could never have been an authentic work of the Holy Spirit, because there is also the possibility that it was rather the refusal of the church of that time to admit its need of reform and accept renewal that led to the alienation and eventual separation.

Needless to say, this is not the place to enter into a discussion of any particular historical cases, with a view to assessing the responsibility for the alienation of renewal movements from the churches they wanted to renew. It is sufficient simply to observe that the history of Western Christianity in the last four hundred years has been profoundly marked by alienations of this kind, whether from the Catholic Church in the sixteenth century, or from various Protestant bodies in the following centuries. If in the past we Catholics tended to judge, rather simplistically, that there could be nothing of the Holy Spirit in movements that eventually resulted in the formation of new Christian denominations, it is clear that our thinking about the operations of the Holy Spirit has to be much more nuanced. With the Second Vatican Council we not only recognize the working of the Holy Spirit in the hearts of individual Christians, of whatever denomination, we also recognize that the Holy Spirit uses the various churches themselves as channels of grace and salvation.[1] "Nor should we forget that whatever is wrought by the grace of the Holy Spirit in the hearts of our separated brethren can contribute to our own edification."[2]

Keeping the foregoing observations in mind, let us now look at a movement which, at its inception at the beginning of this century, intended the renewal of the Methodist and Holiness churches in the United States, but has subsequently given birth not only to many new churches, grouped under the denomination "Pentecostal," but also to the "charismatic renewal," which is affecting, to some extent, practically every major

Christian church today. In my opinion, there are good reasons to justify speaking of this whole phenomenon as the pentecostal movement.

The Pentecostal Movement

I shall begin with a few remarks about terminology. The term "classical pentecostalism" is now generally used to describe the original form of the pentecostal movement, as it is found both in churches that include the word "Pentecostal" in their title, and in many others, such as the Assemblies of God, that do not. The term "neo-pentecostalism" is applied to the pentecostal movement as it has occurred first within Protestant churches, and then within the Catholic Church. But in recent years there has been a general preference, especially among neo-pentecostals, to speak of this as the "charismatic renewal." I shall leave the question of the justification of this term to later on in the discussion.

The question of terminology is more complicated when it comes to describing the participants in the various branches of the pentecostal movement. My intention is to use the word "Pentecostals" only when I am speaking of members of a Pentecostal church. When speaking of Protestants or Catholics who are involved in the pentecostal movement while remaining in their own churches, I shall use the term "neo-pentecostals," and shall speak of neo-pentecostal Episcopalians, Lutherans, Catholics, etc., when I wish to specify the church to which they belong. This terminology is quite appropriate, in my opinion. However, it is more common nowadays, among those who use the term "charismatic renewal," to speak of participants in it as "charismatics," or, more specifically, as "charismatic Episcopalians," "charismatic Catholics," etc. Serious objections have been raised against this practice by sympathetic observers, including no less eminent a theologian than Yves Congar.[3] The problem lies in appropriating the term "charismatic" in such a way that it seems to become an exclusive prerogative of participants in the pentecostal movement, and is implicitly or explicitly denied to all others. Those who do not participate in this movement become the "non-charismatics," and Congar rightly objects to being relegated to that category of Christians.

I agree with Congar that this use of the term "charismatic" is objectionable. The truth of the matter surely is that anyone who has received a charism and is using it to build up the body of Christ can rightly be called "charismatic." Now of course I do not doubt that many participants in the pentecostal movement are genuinely charismatic in this sense. But on the one hand, I do not agree that to be charismatic it is enough simply to be a participant in this movement; and on the other, I am certain that there are a great many genuinely charismatic people who are not participants in it.

My intention, therefore, is to avoid using the term "charismatics" as a designation of Catholics or Protestants who participate in the pentecostal movement. It seems to me preferable to use the term "neo-pentecostals" instead.

Let us now take a look at the various kinds of people who participate in the pentecostal movement.

The Classical Pentecostals

Classical Pentecostalism is a form of fundamentalist, evangelical Protestantism. Pentecostals are fundamentalist in their use and interpretation of the Bible and their uncompromising adherence to the "fundamental" articles of faith which they hold in common with other evangelical Protestants. They are "evangelical" in their insistence on the necessity of an adult conversion experience for salvation and their rejection of the practice of infant baptism. Pentecostalism is an offshoot of the "Holiness" type of religion, which in its turn had its origins in the American variety of Methodism. Perhaps one can best describe Pentecostalism by indicating what it has in common with Holiness religion, and what are its own distinctive characteristics.

Holiness religion, as a distinct type of Protestantism, developed as a movement of revival within American Methodism in the last half of the nineteenth century. Its leaders, who were revivalist preachers, charged the established Methodist Churches with neglecting John Wesley's doctrine of "entire sanctification," a doctrine which they, on the contrary, made the central theme of their preaching. According to this doctrine, Christians who have already had the experience of conversion, and are thus "saved," should aspire to a "second blessing": i.e., a distinct and deeper religious experience which accomplishes their sanctification and enables them to lead lives of moral perfection, untroubled by any "root of sin." Some Holiness preachers described this experience as a "baptism in the Holy Ghost."[4] While this "second blessing" might be an intensely emotional experience for the person receiving it, it was essentially interior and subjective; there was no external sign by which witnesses could be certain that it was taking place.

The generally recognized founder of Pentecostalism, Charles Fox Parham, had previously been a Holiness preacher. In the year 1900 he opened the Bethel Bible School in Topeka, Kansas, with about thirty resident students, both men and women. The only textbook in use in this school was the Bible. Parham's method of instruction was to propose a question, and then set the students to work searching the Bible for all the texts that might provide its answer. Towards the end of 1900 he proposed the question: "What is the scriptural sign of a true baptism in the Holy Ghost?" From the accounts of Pentecost (Acts 2:1-12) and the other "descents of the Holy Spirit" described in the Acts of the Apostles (Acts 10:44-48; 19:1-7), Parham and his students concluded that the one sure scriptural sign of baptism in the Holy Spirit was the gift of speaking with other tongues. A wave of enthusiastic fervor swept through the school; uninterrupted prayer for such a coming of the Holy Spirit was carried on for several days and nights. On January 1, 1901, a student by the name of Agnes Ozman asked Parham to lay his hands on her head while they prayed; when he did so she experienced her "baptism in the Spirit" and began to speak in tongues. Within a few days all the students and Parham himself had a similar experience. The first Pentecostal group had come into being, distinguished from Holiness groups by the conviction that a genuine baptism in the Spirit would be manifested, as at the first Pentecost, by "speaking in other tongues as the Spirit gave utterance" (Acts 2:4). Along with this insistence on the charismatic sign came a shift in the understanding of "baptism in the Holy Spirit." As we have seen, some Holiness preachers had been using this term to describe the "second blessing" which brought about "entire sanctification." Pentecostals, seeing the baptism in the Spirit as a "new Pentecost" for all believers, interpret this in the light of its effects on the Apostles themselves, namely, as a receiving of power for effective witnessing to Christ, along with the charismatic gifts displayed by the Apostles in their ministry. Those Pentecostals who have remained in the Holiness tradition have not renounced their doctrine of the second blessing for sanctification, but for them the "baptism in the Spirit" is a third experience conferring power to witness. For other Pentecostals, whose previous faith had not included the doctrine of entire sanctification, the baptism in the Spirit is the second blessing, subsequent to the saving experience of conversion.

All Pentecostals believe that the experience of the first disciples on the day of Pentecost was also the normal experience of all believers in the early church, and that all believers even now are entitled to and should earnestly seek a similar experience. They further believe that, as at Pentecost, this "baptism in the Holy Spirit" should be manifested by the sign of glossolalia. They distinguish between glossolalia as the initial sign of Spirit-baptism, and the subsequent, lasting gift of speaking in tongues, which not all receive. Most classical Pentecostals do not recognize a genuine baptism in the Spirit unless it is accompanied by this sign.

From its modest beginnings in Topeka, Pentecostalism spread to Texas, and thence, in 1906, to Los Angeles, where it enjoyed phenomenal success under the leadership of a black former Holiness preacher, William J. Seymour. I shall not recount the history of its growth and expansion throughout the United States, where it now numbers more than two million adherents. A few observations seem especially worth making.

First, it was not the intention of Parham, Seymour, and the early Pentecostal leaders to found a new Christian denomination. Their aim was rather to bring about a revival within their respective churches. It was only when they were rejected by their churches that they began to form their own separate congregations. On the other hand, some Holiness churches accepted the new teaching about baptism in the Spirit as a "third blessing," and became the first of the "Pentecostal-Holiness" churches.

Second, Pentecostalism, in its relatively brief history, has given rise to an astonishing number of distinct churches. According to the Pentecostal historian, Vinson Synan, by the year 1925 there were thirty-eight Pentecostal denominations in the United States alone.[5] He groups them into three major "families," on the basis of certain points of doctrine on which they differ from one another: the Holiness-Pentecostal bodies, which retain the teaching about entire sanctification; the Assemblies of God and other Pentecostal bodies, which accept only the distinctively Pentecostal baptism in the Spirit as a "second blessing"; and the "Jesus Only" groups, which teach that there is only one person who is God, namely, Jesus Christ. The other two groups retain the traditional doctrine of the Trinity.

Pentecostalism spread to Europe as early as 1906, first to the Scandinavian countries, and later to Great Britain and the continent. It has subsequently spread to all parts of the world, and in recent decades has outstripped all other Christian denominations in its rate of growth, especially in Latin America and Africa. Pentecostal evangelism has had phenomenal success in almost every country in Latin America. Damboriena estimates the number of Pentecostals in the Central American and Caribbean areas at close to half a million; in Chile at about a million, and in any case about eighty percent of the Protestant population; and in Brazil at up to four million.[6]

Neo-Pentecostal Protestants

The past two decades have seen an outbreak of pentecostalism within the older Protestant churches, mainly in the United States, but also in Europe and other parts of the world. Neo-pentecostal Protestants, while they remain communicating members of their own churches, participate in prayer groups, whose members have already received or aspire to the "baptism in the Spirit," with the accompanying sign of tongues. Because of the notoriety attached to this phenomenon, neo-pentecostalism has often been referred to as the "tongues movement." Protestant pastors have played an important role in introducing this movement into their churches; among the best known of these are Dennis Bennett (Episcopalian), Harald Bredesen (Reformed), Larry Christenson (Lutheran), and Rodney Willians (Presbyterian) in the United States, and Michael Harper (Anglican) in England. Neo-pentecostal Protestants are usually faithful participants in the regular Sunday worship of their churches, but they also meet during the week, either in the church or a private home, for a pentecostal type of prayer meeting. If their pastor is in a group, he may also be its leader; otherwise a lay member of the group will be recognized to have the charism of leadership.

For the most part, the initial reaction of the governing bodies of the Protestant churches in the United States was rather negative to the outbreak of the pentecostal movement among their clergy and faithful. In some cases, pastors were removed or forced to resign as a result of their encouraging this movement among their people. However, in recent years the governing bodies of several important Protestant churches in the United States have issued statements much more favorable to what is now more often being referred to as the "charismatic renewal" in their churches.[7]

Neo-Pentecostal Catholics:
The Catholic Charismatic Renewal

Neo-pentecostal Protestants provided the bridge across the chasm that had previously separated Pentecostals and Catholics. The reading of two books about Pentecostalism[8] led four Catholic lay faculty members at Duquesne University to seek out a group of neo-pentecostal Protestants in a Pittsburgh suburb, so that they might learn from them how to receive the "baptism in the Spirit." After attending several prayer meetings with this group, two of the Catholics asked that they might be prayed for and have hands laid on them by the members of the group; when this was done they had the typical pentecostal experience and began to speak in tongues. They shared their experience with a group of Catholic students during a weekend retreat in February, 1967, with the result that the first Catholic neo-pentecostal prayer group came into existence, and significantly, at a Catholic university.[9] From there the movement spread to Notre Dame and other universities, and to parishes, convents, and monasteries in all parts of the United States and Canada. In those earliest years there were many who thought that this would remain a peculiarly North American phenomenon, not suited to other cultures, but events were quickly to prove them wrong. Less than seven years after the first Catholic group was formed, an International Leaders' Conference of the Catholic Charismatic Renewal was held in Grottaferrata, on the outskirts of Rome, attended by the leaders of prayer groups in thirty-four countries. At Pentecost, during the Holy Year of 1975, an International Congress of the Renewal was held in Rome itself, to which 10,000 participants came from over sixty countries in all parts of the world. The Fourth International Leaders' Conference, held in Rome in May 1981 was attended by leaders of the Catholic renewal from ninety-four countries.

Neo-pentecostal Catholics, while acknowledging their indebtedness to classical Pentecostalism, have not left the Catholic Church in significant numbers to join one of the Pentecostal Churches. On the contrary, the evidence seems convincing that they have generally become more faithful participants in the life of the church as a result of their pentecostal experience. Besides their regular attendance at the parish liturgy, they also belong to a prayer group, which usually meets once a week in a private home, a church hall, retreat house, or other suitable place. Such meetings consist of scripture readings, hymns, prayer, both intelligible and in tongues, the giving of testimony, a homily or instruction, and the like.

If one asks in what respect the meetings of a neo-pentecostal Catholic group differ from those of any other group that meets for shared prayer, I would mention the following as its distinctive characteristics.

First, the emphasis on praise as the primary attitude of prayer. This creates and sustains an atmosphere of prayer that is centered on God, rather than on the personal needs of the participants. Joyful, enthusiastic praising of God, often in song, is typical of these meetings.

The second distinctive feature is the likelihood that during the meeting there will be moments when the whole group will be praising God vocally, each in his or her own words, and that at such times at least some in the group will be praying in tongues. In many groups such moments of vocal prayer will turn into spontaneous "singing in the Spirit," with each person forming his or her own melody, either using real words or in tongues. Many groups produce a strangely beautiful harmony in such singing.

A third feature is the likelihood that someone will "prophesy," that is, speak a message as coming from God to the group. In most cases, such prophecies will be biblical in content and style, and will be consoling or exhortative rather than predictive.

But the most distinctive characteristic of a neo-pentecostal meeting is the likelihood that during it there will be some mention of being "baptized in the Spirit." The nucleus of any such group will be made up of people who know what it has meant to them to have been "baptized in the Spirit," and who are eager to share this blessing with others. Indeed, the sharing of this experience is at the very heart of the charismatic renewal. And so we shall now take a close look at what people mean when they talk about being "baptized in the Spirit."

FIVE

"Baptism in the Spirit"

IN MY OPINION, the remarkable growth of the charismatic renewal in the Catholic Church can be explained only in reference to the experience that so many people have had of lives that have been changed after they have been prayed with for a new outpouring of the Spirit, or, as most of them will put it, after having been "baptized in the Spirit."

What these people actually experienced were the changes that took place in their lives. To attribute those changes to a "release of the Spirit," to a "new outpouring of the Spirit," or to "being baptized in the Spirit" is to offer a theological explanation of the cause of what has happened to them. Looking rather at the experience than at varying interpretations of it, there are reasons to speak of it as "pentecostal," because in many respects it resembles the experience of the first disciples at Pentecost. Jesus promised the Eleven that they would receive power and be his witnesses through the coming of the Holy Spirit upon them (Acts 1:8). And we see how they were transformed from weak, fearful men into bold apostles, unafraid to announce the Gospel to the very people who had put Jesus to death.

In our time, many people can testify to something similar happening to them. They know that a new power to live their Christian commitment and to witness to their faith has come into their lives. Like the first disciples, very many find themselves moved in a new way to the praise of God, even beyond their power to express this praise in words. They testify to a new sense of the reality of the Lord whom they meet in their prayer, to a totally new realization of what it means that "Jesus is Lord." And therefore, like the disciples at Pentecost, they want nothing more than to share their experience with others.

The message that people involved in the charismatic renewal wish to proclaim to all who will listen is really the same good news that Peter announced for the first time at Pentecost: that Jesus is Lord, that he has poured out his Spirit, and that he will give the same Spirit to all who repent of their sins and accept him as their Lord.

While the message of the charismatic renewal is that given by Peter, most of the hearers now are different, being Christians who have already received the Holy Spirit at their baptism. So now the crucial question is whether there is any sense in saying to baptized Christians: "Repent, accept Jesus as your Lord, and you shall receive the gift of the Holy Spirit."

It is important to understand that the experience comes first, and theological interpretations follow afterward. What people in the charismatic renewal have experienced is that when already baptized Christians respond to this message in a new way, when they wish really to accept Jesus as the Lord of their lives, and then ask others to pray with them for a "baptism in the Holy Spirit," real changes very often do take place which suggest that the Holy Spirit is indeed at work in them in a new, more evident, and more powerful way.

I believe that such experiences, which are both widespread and well attested, justify us in concluding that there is in fact a sense in which the promise of Acts 2:38 applies also to baptized Christians. Obviously, they cannot receive the sacrament of baptism again. But, "to be baptized in the name of Jesus" means to commit oneself to him as one's Lord.

It is quite possible that a person who was baptized as an infant has never personally ratified the Christian commitment that was made for him by others at his christening. It is quite possible that the sacrament of confirmation did not involve any deep personal commitment either. In such a case, which surely is not so uncommon, I think one is correct in saying that a person's Christian initiation still needs to be completed. Even though it is complete sacramentally, there is still something lacking in regard to his personal ratification or appropriation of what was done to him.

Furthermore, I believe that one can rightly speak of various levels or degrees of personal appropriation of sacramental initiation. There can be a great difference, for instance, between the depth of personal decision involved in an adolescent reception of confirmation, and the kind of profound conversion that one can experience in the *Spiritual Exercises* of St. Ignatius or in the charismatic renewal.

The conviction of people involved in the charismatic renewal that the promise of Acts 2:38 has a meaning also for baptized Christians is the fruit of their experience. They know that when Christians hear the Gospel anew, wish to accept Jesus as the Lord of their lives in a radical way, and ask him to "baptize them in the Spirit," things do begin to happen to them which suggest a new presence and working of the Holy Spirit in their lives.

Needless to say, they are not receiving the Holy Spirit for the first time. But if this is the first time someone has made a really personal decision to live as a Christian, I think we may speak of it as the completion of his Christian initiation. If he has made such a decision before, but is now making it at a deeper, more total level, it is still reasonable to think that prayer made with such dispositions will be answered. In any case, what a great many baptized Christians know is that after such prayer, changes have taken place in their lives which they feel sure are not their own doing, and indeed are such that they can only attribute them to God.

But one might ask: even granted that genuine conversions do take place, even granted that people really are changed, is it in accord with Catholic tradition to attribute such effects as these to a "being baptized in the Spirit"? Is not the Holy Spirit given to us in the sacraments? Can we speak of any subsequent, non-sacramental event in a Christian's life as a "being baptized in the Holy Spirit"?

Let us see how Catholics involved in the charismatic renewal have answered these questions.

Catholic Explanations of "Baptism in the Spirit"

When Catholics began to share the pentecostal experience, they generally accepted the term "baptism in the Spirit" to describe it, but they realized that they had to make it clear that this in no way conflicted with Catholic belief that the Holy Spirit was already given in the sacraments of baptism and confirmation. Above all they wanted to avoid giving the impression that they now looked on sacramental baptism as a mere "baptism in water," as though it was only through a pentecostal experience that a person really received the Holy Spirit.

The solution which has been most commonly adopted in the literature of the Catholic charismatic renewal is to see the "giving" or "imparting" of the Holy Spirit as taking place exclusively in the sacraments. There is an evident reluctance to speak of a new imparting of the Spirit except through the reception of a sacrament, as though this would be incompatible with Catholic theology.

How then have Catholics explained what happens when people are "baptized in the Spirit" in the charismatic renewal? The most representative answer to this question, in some sense expressing a consensus of opinion among leaders in the Catholic renewal, is found in the first of what are called the "Malines Documents."[1] Here are the most pertinent passages of this document regarding the question I have raised.

Within the Catholic renewal the phrase "baptism in the Holy Spirit" refers to two senses or moments. First, there is the theological sense. In this sense, every member of the Church has been baptized in the Spirit because each has received sacramental initiation. Second, there is the experiential sense. It refers to the moment or the growth process in virtue of which the Spirit, given during the celebration of initiation, comes to conscious experience. When those within the Catholic renewal speak of "the baptism in the Holy Spirit" they are ordinarily referring to this conscious experience, which is the experiential sense.[2]

If Roman Catholics use the phrase "baptism in the Spirit" they ordinarily mean something different from what those involved in renewal movements outside the Roman Church believe. Classical Pentecostals and Protestant neo-pentecostals generally use the phrase to indicate a second blessing posterior to conversion, a new imparting of the Spirit. In most cases it is not related to any sacramental context. On the other hand, when Roman Catholics use the phrase it usually means the breaking forth into conscious experience of the Spirit who was given during the celebration of initiation.[3]

As I see it, the key to this explanation of what is happening in the charismatic renewal is the distinction between the "theological" and the "experiential" sense in which one can be said to be "baptized in the Spirit." According to this distinction, people are baptized in the Spirit in the theological sense in sacramental initiation, whereas what happens in the charismatic renewal involves only the experiential sense of this term. "Baptism in the Spirit" in the theological sense is understood as a real imparting of the Spirit, whereas in the experiential sense there is only a "coming into the conscious experience of the power of the Spirit already received."

Perhaps the best way to express my own opinion on this question is to say that I believe that what happens to people in the charismatic renewal is that they are baptized in the Spirit in the *biblical* sense of this term, and that *the biblical sense includes both the theological and the experiential senses.* In other words, in my view, what people are receiving in the charismatic renewal is a real imparting of the Spirit, a new "outpouring of the Spirit" (the theological sense), which typically has effects that make them aware that the Spirit is working in a new way in their lives (the experiential sense).

First I shall explain why I call this the "biblical sense" of the term, and second I shall explain why I believe it is consonant with Catholic theology to understand "baptism in the Spirit" in this way. For the biblical sense of this expression, let us see how it is used, first in the Gospels, and then in the Acts of the Apostles.

The Meaning of "Baptize in the Spirit" in the Gospels

While all four evangelists attribute to John the Baptist the prophecy that Jesus would "baptize in the Holy Spirit," there is good reason to believe that Matthew and Luke are our best witnesses as to what he himself most probably meant by his prophecy. Whereas Mark and John have the Baptist say merely that Jesus would "baptize in the Holy Spirit,"[4] Matthew and Luke report his words as "He will baptize you in the Holy Spirit and fire."[5] Furthermore, it is only these two Gospels that give us the context that explains what he most likely meant by this saying. This context is the preaching of the Baptist about the imminent judgment which the "one mightier than he" was going to execute upon all who refused to prepare for his coming by repentance for their sins. This context, as well as the use of the terms "spirit" and "fire" in similar contexts in the Old Testament, show that in the intention of John the Baptist the contrast he drew between his own baptizing in water and the coming one's "baptizing in the holy spirit and fire" was the contrast between a purifying act of repentance that prepared people for the judgment, and the purifying judgment itself that would cleanse the whole people and condemn those who failed to repent.[6]

When we turn from Matthew and Luke to Mark and John, we see that the latter have omitted not only the mention of "fire," but the whole context of the Baptist's preaching about the imminent judgment. Here it would seem clear that we are dealing with a later Christian interpretation of the Baptist's prophecy, as no longer a warning of messianic judgment, but a promise of the messianic outpouring of the Holy Spirit, which had already been predicted by the prophets of the Old Testament.[7]

"Baptized in the Spirit" in Acts

That such was in fact the Christian interpretation of the Baptist's prophecy is put beyond all doubt by the two texts of Acts in which Luke tells us how this prophecy was fulfilled.[8] In both texts, the saying appears as a promise spoken by Jesus himself, and in both, the promise is seen to be fulfilled in the outpouring of the Holy Spirit on the disciples at Pentecost. In the second text, it is seen to be fulfilled also in the coming of the Spirit on the household of Cornelius. Since these two passages of Acts are the clearest and most explicit witnesses to the meaning which this term had for New Testament Christians, we shall now examine these texts more closely, to determine just what Luke meant by "being baptized in the Holy Spirit."

The first point to notice is that the fulfillment of the promise that the disciples of Jesus would be baptized in the Spirit is seen not in a literal baptism in water that would also be a "baptism in the Spirit," but rather in a coming of the Holy Spirit in which there is no mention of the sacrament of baptism (Pentecost), or one which takes place prior to the conferring of the sacrament (as in the case of Cornelius).

The conclusion seems obvious that the word "baptize" is being used here in a figurative sense. If so, what meaning does it have? A look at a standard dictionary of New Testament Greek shows that the basic meaning of the word *baptizo* was "dip, immerse, plunge, sink, drench." This suggests that to say, "You will be baptized in the Holy Spirit," is equivalent to saying, "You will be immersed in, drenched with, the Holy Spirit." In other words, we are dealing with substantially the same metaphor that underlies the more common biblical expression for giving the Spirit, namely, to "pour out" the Spirit.[9]

If we look at the other passages in which Luke has referred to these two events, in which he saw the fulfillment of the promise that Jesus would baptize his disciples in the Holy Spirit,[10] we see that he has used a variety of verbs, which give us a good idea of his understanding of what it meant to be "baptized in the Spirit." As synonyms for "baptize in the Spirit" he has used "to send," "to pour out," "to give" the Spirit; equivalent expressions for "being baptized in the Spirit" are "being clothed with," "receiving," "being filled with" the Spirit, and having the Spirit "come" or "fall upon" one. To say that Jesus "baptizes" in the Holy Spirit, then, is simply a biblical metaphor for saying that he sends or gives us the Spirit. To "be baptized in the Spirit" is to receive an outpouring of the Spirit, or, more literally, to receive the gift of the Spirit.

The Experiential Aspect of New Testament "Baptism in the Spirit"

If "being baptized in the Spirit" in the theological sense means that there is a real imparting and receiving of the Spirit, there can be no doubt that the biblical sense of this term includes the theological sense. I have said above that the biblical sense also includes the experiential sense. What I mean by this is that when people received the gift of the Holy Spirit in the New Testament, they became consciously aware of the working of the Spirit in their lives. Let us look at some of the evidence of this that we find in the New Testament.

First, we have the two events in which Luke explicitly recognized the fulfillment of the promise that Jesus would baptize his disciples in the Holy Spirit. It hardly seems necessary to point out the experiential character of these receptions of the Spirit. But it would be a great mistake to identify the disciples' experience of the power of the Spirit at work in them only with their immediate outburst of praise in tongues. Undoubtedly Luke intends to describe the ongoing experience of the presence of the Spirit in the primitive Christian community when he tells us: "And fear came upon every soul; and many wonders and signs were done through the apostles. And all who believed were together and had all things in common; and they sold their possessions and goods and distributed them to all, as any had need. And day by day, attending the temple together and breaking bread in their homes, they partook of food with glad and generous hearts, praising God and having favor with all the people" (Acts 2:43-47).

Later on, when the Holy Spirit "fell" upon Cornelius and his household, the effects of his presence were evident not only to the recipients but to Peter and his companions as well. That some such experiential evidence of the outpouring of the Spirit was normal and expected in New Testament times provides the answer to the question how the Apostles knew that the Holy Spirit "had not fallen" on the Samaritans whom Philip had baptized (Acts 8:16). When these people did receive the Spirit, Luke tells us that Simon "saw that the Spirit was given through the laying on of the Apostles' hands" (Acts 8:18). How could he have "seen" this, except that the Samaritans now began to show evidence of the power of the Spirit at work in them? Again, the most likely explanation of St. Paul's question to the twelve disciples whom he met at Ephesus, "Did you receive the Holy Spirit when you believed?" is that he did not find in them the evidence that he expected to find in Christians who had received the Spirit. When the Holy Spirit did come upon them, the experiential element was again forthcoming: "When Paul had laid his hands upon them the Holy Spirit came on them, and they spoke with tongues and prophesied" (Acts 19:6).

The examples we have seen so far are all from Acts. But the letters of St. Paul also testify that the power of the Spirit was a matter of experience for the Christians of his day. One of the clearest indications of this is his appeal to the Galatians: "Let me ask you only this: Did you receive the Spirit by works of the law, or by hearing with faith? Are you so foolish? Having begun with the Spirit, are you now ending with the flesh? Did you experience so many things in vain?—if it really is in vain. Does he who supplies the Spirit to you and works miracles among you do so by works of the law, or by hearing with faith?" (Gal 3:2-5). Paul bases his argument here on the fact that the Galatians' life as Christians was marked from the very beginning by their experience of the power of the Holy Spirit. He knew that he could appeal to their consciousness of the Spirit's power at work in and among them; it was not something that they had to simply take on faith.

I think that these examples are enough to justify the assertion that "baptism in the Spirit" in the New Testament was not only a real imparting of the gift of the Spirit (the theological sense), but also meant a becoming aware of the power of the Spirit at work in those who received the Spirit (the experiential sense).

It is time now to give my reasons for thinking that what is happening to many people in the charismatic renewal is also a "baptism in the Spirit" in the biblical sense, by which I mean that it includes both the theological and the experiential aspects.

First, a word about the experiential sense. I do not know of anyone who disagrees with the assertion that "baptism in the Spirit," as a distinctive feature of the whole pentecostal movement, is understood to involve some new awareness of the power of the Spirit in one's life. In this broad sense, at least, I think everyone agrees that it is "experiential." But a further question, to which different answers are given, is whether there is any particular kind of experiential evidence that one should look for, to show that a real "baptism in the Spirit" has taken place. As we have seen earlier, it is the belief of most Pentecostals that there is such a particular kind of evidence, namely, speaking in tongues.

Now it can hardly be denied that the belief that a genuine "baptism in the Spirit" ought to be manifested by the sign of tongues has had great influence on the whole pentecostal movement. However, the first "Malines Document," expressing the consensus of leaders in the Catholic charismatic renewal, asserts: "It is now generally recognized that what is called "baptism in the Spirit' is not in any way tied to tongues."[11] In fact, this same document expresses the view that the "coming into conscious experience" of the power of the

Spirit can take place by way of a "growth process," and need not be a matter of immediate experience. I am in agreement with this document on both of these points.

Therefore I shall move on to the question on which I differ with the view expressed in the Malines Document, namely, whether we Catholics can understand what people are receiving in the charismatic renewal as a real imparting of the Spirit: in other words, whether it is a "baptism in the Spirit" in the theological sense, and not *merely* in the experiential sense.

The position taken in the document, which we have quoted earlier, strikes me as dictated by the apprehension that there might be something alien to Catholic faith in recognizing any giving or receiving of the Holy Spirit except in and through the sacraments. It seems to suspect as unorthodox the idea that one could receive a new sending of the Spirit in answer to a prayer that was not a sacrament.

Second, it suggests the idea, if it does not express it, that in sacramental initiation we receive a "total gift of the Spirit," so that there can be no further question of receiving the Spirit, but only of "coming into conscious experience" of the Spirit already sacramentally imparted.

Here are some reflections of mine on this approach to the question. First, it does not seem to me to be consonant with traditional Catholic theology to think that in the sacraments of initiation we receive a "total gift of the Spirit," including all the graces and charisms that we are ever going to have, and that subsequently all that happens is that some or all of these gifts "break through into conscious experience." I do not see how such a theory is compatible with a Catholic understanding of what happens in such a sacrament as Holy Orders, which surely is traditionally understood to involve a new sending of the Spirit with new gifts. St. Paul, for instance, urges Timothy not to neglect the gift that was given him with the laying on of hands (1 Tm 4:14).

Second, I do not think that the fact of the power of the Spirit, hitherto unexperienced, becoming a matter of personal conscious experience, can be explained merely as a change in my subjective consciousness. Rather, it seems to me that if I become conscious of the power of the Spirit in me, it is because the Spirit really begins to work in me in a new way, such that I am really changed. Now to say that the Holy Spirit begins to work new effects of grace in me, theologically involves saying that he is present in me in a new way. And if he is present in me in a new way, this means that there must have been a new "sending" of the Spirit, because the Spirit is present in us precisely as "sent" by the Father and Son.

Third, I do not believe that there is anything in Catholic theology that obliges us to believe that new "sendings" of the Holy Spirit can take place only through the reception of a sacrament. In fact, I believe that I have the support of no less an authority than St. Thomas Aquinas for my view that real "sendings" of the Spirit take place when people are "baptized in the Spirit." His teaching throws a great deal of light on this question, so I shall briefly summarize it here.

St. Thomas Aquinas on the "Sendings" of the Spirit

The first point he makes is that when we talk about the sending of a Divine Person, we cannot think of this as a real movement from one place to another, or as a becoming present where the Person was not at all present before. So it must be a question of the Divine Person becoming present where he is already, by a new kind of presence. This new kind of presence cannot involve a real change in God; hence it must be understood by reason of a real change in the creature to whom he becomes present. The creature must begin to have a new relationship to the Divine Person, a relationship that involves a new way of being united with God, so that God is truly present in him in a new way. The two key words which for St. Thomas express what happens when the Holy Spirit is given or sent to us are *inhabitation* and *innovation*: the Holy Spirit *dwells* in us, in such a way as to *make us new*. [12]

Now, of course, in Catholic teaching this takes place initially at the moment when we become Christians, when we are "born of water and the Spirit" (Jn 3:5). But St. Thomas also asks the question whether we can speak of a sending of the Spirit to a person in whom he is already indwelling, and if so, how this is to be understood. His answer is as follows: "There is an invisible sending also with respect to an advance in virtue or an increase of grace. . . . Such an invisible sending is especially to be seen in that kind of increase of grace whereby a person moves forward into some new act or some new state of grace: as, for instance, when a person moves forward into the grace of working miracles, or of prophecy, or out of the burning love of God offers his life as a martyr, or renounces all his possessions, or undertakes some other such arduous thing."[13]

Several points in this text deserve comment. First, we know from a previous work of St. Thomas that he was aware that some medieval theologians held that there was a new sending of the Spirit whenever there was an increase of grace or virtue in the soul. St. Thomas did not reject this view outright, but he prefers to speak of such a new sending of the Divine Person where it is a question of a decisively new work of grace, such as can be described as "moving into a new act or new state of grace."[14] Second, this is in keeping with his insistence that a new sending of the Spirit must involve a real "innovation" in the person in whom the Spirit begins to dwell in a new way. And finally, when we look at the "new acts" or "new states" of grace which he gives as examples of the fruit of such a new sending of the Spirit, we do not find the kinds of grace which are traditionally attributed to the reception of sacraments. All of the examples he gives would fall under the heading of charismatic, rather than sacramental, graces. And there is nothing in the context that would in any way suggest that a new sending of the Spirit, with such effects as these, could only be had through the reception of a sacrament.

I conclude from this teaching of St. Thomas that there is no reason why Catholics, who believe that they have already received the Holy Spirit in their sacramental initiation, should not look forward to new "sendings" of the Spirit to them, which would move them from the "state of grace" in which they already are into some "new act" or "new state of grace." Now if we recall that in biblical language, "sending the Spirit," "pouring out the Spirit," and "baptizing in the Spirit" are simply different ways of saying the same thing, the conclusion follows that it is quite in accord with traditional Catholic theology for baptized and confirmed Christians to ask the Lord to "baptize them in the Holy Spirit." What they are asking him for, in the language of St. Thomas, is a new "sending" of the Holy Spirit, which would begin a decisively new work of grace in their lives. As we have seen from the examples which St. Thomas gives, he would obviously not be surprised if such a new work of grace involved a charismatic gift.

However, it must be noted that if we follow the lead of St. Thomas, we cannot interpret the new sending of the Spirit as simply the conferring of a charism. As he explains it, a new sending of the Spirit must involve a new way of the Spirit's indwelling in the soul, and this has to mean a real *innovation* of the person's relationship with the indwelling Spirit. Therefore, in Thomas' view, it has to mean a more intimate and "experiential" knowledge of God as present in the soul, a knowledge that "breaks out into more ardent love."[15]

Some Further Conclusions from the Teaching of St. Thomas

If we interpret what people in the charismatic renewal are calling "baptism in the Spirit" in the light of what St. Thomas calls "sendings of the Spirit that move people into some new act or new state of grace," several further conclusions follow which I shall mention briefly here.

First, there is good reason to believe that such new "sendings of the Spirit" or "baptisms in the Spirit" have been happening to people all through Christian history. The life-story of practically any holy person, canonized or not, will usually include some turning-point, some conversion, that marked a decisive change in that person's life. This is the sort of thing that St. Ignatius expected to happen to people who made the thirty days of the Spiritual Exercises, and surely Ignatian retreats have borne this kind of fruit many times during the past four hundred years. Ignatius tells us that what he wanted to happen during the Exercises was that "the Creator and Lord in person communicate Himself to the devout soul in quest of the divine will, that He inflame it with His love and praise, and dispose it for the way in which it could better serve God in the future."[16]

When we read a passage like this in the Exercises, we can only ask why St. Ignatius does not speak explicitly of the Holy Spirit as the uncreated Gift by which God communicates himself in person to the soul. Very likely his reticence about the Holy Spirit in the book of the Exercises is to be explained by his care not to say anything that could arouse suspicion of Illuminism. But there is no reason now why we should not recognize the Holy Spirit in those passages of the Exercises in which St. Ignatius speaks of "the Creator and Lord communicating Himself to the soul, inflaming it with His love and praise," or where he says that "it belongs solely to the Creator to come into a soul, to leave it, to act upon it, to draw it wholly to the love of the Divine Majesty."[17]

The second point I would make is that there is no reason to think that a "new sending of the Spirit," or a "baptism in the Spirit" could take place only once in a person's lifetime. It is true, of course, that the use of the expression "baptism in the Spirit" can create the impression that, like the sacrament of baptism, this must be a kind of initiation, an unrepeatable, once-in-a-lifetime event. But, to my way of thinking, this is just one of the reasons why the term "baptism in the Spirit" is open to misunderstanding on the part of people who are accustomed to speak of "baptism" only in connection with the sacrament. Another source of misunderstanding is the fact that in the case of the sacrament, it is correct to say that the priest baptizes, because he does confer the sacrament. But when we use the term "baptize in the Spirit" in the charismatic renewal, we are using it as a synonym for "send the Spirit" or "pour out the Spirit." In this case, it is only Jesus who really "baptizes in the Spirit," because it is his unique glory, as the risen Lord, to receive from the Father the gift of the Spirit and to pour it out on his disciples.[18] It is not the people who gather around and pray for someone who "baptize him or her in the Spirit"; it is the Lord who does this, in answer to their prayer.

Another possible misunderstanding is to attribute to this prayer the kind of efficacy that we are accustomed to attribute to the sacrament of baptism. I do not think it is correct to say that if a person has been "prayed over" for the "baptism in the Spirit," he can be assured that he has really been "baptized in the Spirit," if neither he nor anyone else can subsequently detect any change in him that could even remotely be described as a "new act or new state of grace." When a person is sacramentally baptized, we have the assurance of our faith that he or she has been moved into the "state of grace." We do not need any experiential confirmation of this, nor are we accustomed to expect any, since most often the recipient of the sacrament is an infant. But if "baptism in the Spirit" means coming into some new experience of the power of the Spirit in one's life, then I do not see how a person can be said to have been "baptized in the Spirit," in this sense, unless there is some kind of experienced change in that person's Christian life.

Needless to say, I do not believe that this experiential element *has* to include speaking in tongues; if this were so, I could hardly maintain my opinion that such "baptisms in the Spirit" have been taking place all through Christian history.

One final word about terminology. Throughout this chapter I have used the term "baptism in the Spirit" because this is the term that is most commonly used, at least in the English-speaking world. But I have just mentioned a number of misunderstandings to which this term can lead because of its association with the sacrament of baptism. It is true that there is biblical warrant for the metaphorical use of this term, but I prefer to use another equally biblical metaphor, and to speak rather of a new "outpouring of the Spirit."[19] But if, as seems likely, the term "baptism in the Spirit" is here to stay, I suggest that at any rate we avoid speaking of it as "*the* baptism in the Spirit," as though this were the *only* event in a person's life that could rightly be called by that name. It would be better to speak of praying for a "new baptism in the Spirit," or even better, to say that we are asking the Lord to "baptize someone anew in his Holy Spirit."

To speak of praying for a "new outpouring of the Spirit" would also help correct the impression that "baptism in the Spirit" is a once-in-a-lifetime event. I am convinced that there will never be a time during our pilgrimage on earth when the Lord could not give us a powerful new gift of his Spirit that would really move us into some new act or new state of grace.

In the next chapter we are going to reflect on the fact (attested by St. Thomas) that such a new act or new state of grace might well be "charismatic," and we shall see what people mean when they talk about "charismatic renewal."

SIX

"Charismatic Renewal"

W E HAVE SEEN that when St. Thomas gave examples of the "new acts" or "new states of grace" into which a person could be moved by a new sending of the Spirit, he named the grace of working miracles, of prophecy, of offering one's life as a martyr, and of renouncing all one's possessions. There is a striking parallel between these gifts of grace mentioned by St. Thomas, and the charisms which St. Paul listed at the beginning of 1 Corinthians 13: "If I have prophetic powers, . . . if I have faith so as to remove mountains, . . . if I give away all I have, . . . if I deliver my body to be burned . . ." (1 Cor 13:2-3). It is evident that St. Thomas judged it likely that a new sending of the Holy Spirit would result in a person's receiving some charismatic grace.

Now if, as I believe, "baptism in the Spirit" is really the same sort of thing that St. Thomas called a "new sending of the Spirit," it follows that people in the charismatic renewal have firm support from traditional Catholic theology for their belief that being "baptized in the Spirit" is likely to be the beginning of some charismatic working of the Spirit in one's life. Of course they did not come to this conclusion by a process of theological reasoning. They simply found by experience that this is what happens, and so they have come to expect it to happen. My point here is that there is good theological warrant for thinking that this is the sort of thing that one can rightly expect to happen when a person receives a new outpouring of the Spirit.

We might reflect for a moment on why this is so. It seems to me that one reason is that we are talking about a new sending of the Spirit to people in whom the Spirit is already indwelling. This means that they already have the gifts of grace that make them pleasing to God (*gratiae gratum facientes*) such as sanctifying grace, the theological virtues of faith, hope, and love, and the "seven gifts" of the Spirit. Of course a new outpouring of the Spirit can, and indeed ought to, mean an increase in some or all of these gifts, especially a more ardent love of God. But since they already have all of these gifts in some measure, it is not surprising that when the Holy Spirit begins to do something decisively new in them, to work an "innovation," to "move them into a new act or new state of grace," he will give them another *kind* of grace, the kind traditionally called *gratiae gratis datae,* namely, charismatic grace.

Another reason why a new sending of the Spirit is likely to mean the giving of a charismatic grace is that charisms, as St. Paul tells us, are "manifestations of the Spirit for a useful purpose" (1 Cor 12:7). The reason for a new sending of the Spirit to a person in whom the Spirit is already indwelling can very well be the intention of God to make this person "able and willing to undertake some task or service advantageous for the renewal and upbuilding of the Church."[1]

Just as Pentecost was followed by the Apostles' discovery of their charismatic power to convert multitudes, to stand up and confess the name of Jesus before the Sanhedrin, to suffer joyfully for his name, to heal the sick and to raise the dead, so also, throughout Christian history, men and women have had "pentecostal" experiences which marked for them also the beginning of their charismatic gifts. For instance, we speak of the charism of the founder or foundress of a religious order or congregation. Do we not find, in the lives of most such people, a decisive moment of conversion, a time of "being taken hold of by God," that marked the beginning of their charism for founding a new community in the church? Can we not speak of this as their "pentecostal experience," or their "baptism in the Spirit," followed by their discovery that they had a new gift of the Spirit for some kind of service in the church? Indeed, would not the origin of many individual vocations to ministry in the priesthood or the religious life (charisms in the truest sense of the word) show a similar pattern?

There is, then, an intrinsic connection between "pentecostal" events (new sendings of the Spirit, "baptisms in the Spirit") and charismatic gifts, because the former mark the beginning of a new presence and working of the Holy Spirit, and the latter are "manifestations" of that new presence "for a useful purpose." In other words, if a movement is genuinely "pentecostal," it is normal that it should also be "charismatic."

Lest there be any misunderstanding, I must insist that when I use the word "pentecostal" here, I do not limit it to an experience or movement that is characterized by speaking in tongues. I see no more reason to insist on that particular detail of the first Pentecost than on others such as the sound of rushing wind, or the visible tongues of fire. When I say that a movement that is "pentecostal" will also be "charismatic," I use these terms in a way that I believe applies to all the great charismatic movements in the history of the church.

"Charismatic Renewal"

In a previous chapter I remarked that Catholics involved in this movement have adopted the term "charismatic renewal" in preference to such earlier terms as "Catholic Pentecostalism" or "the Pentecostal Movement in the Catholic Church."[2] While, for reasons that I have already explained, I think it is unfortunate that this has resulted in the common practice of speaking of participants in this renewal as "the charismatics," I am convinced that there are good reasons for describing the movement as a charismatic renewal. I shall now give the reasons why I am convinced of this.

First, if, as I believe, the Second Vatican Council accomplished a renewal of Catholic *theory* about charisms, it is also true that the past decade or so has witnessed a renewal of the *experience* of charisms in the Catholic Church. I do not, of course, imply that there had been a lack of charisms in the church before this time; but it can hardly be denied that what Vatican II taught about charisms "being distributed among the faithful of every rank" has in recent years become a lived experience for hundreds of thousands of Catholics as it had never been before. I think it would be true to say that before 1967 few Catholics would have thought of praying for charisms (except perhaps for "vocations," which they probably would not have thought of calling charisms). And yet the theological grounds for praying for charisms were already implicit in the teaching of Vatican II about the usefulness of such gifts for the renewal and upbuilding of the church. Since Catholics began to pray to be "baptized in the Spirit," there has been a renewal of expectant prayer for charisms, of openness to receiving them, of appreciation of their usefulness. In the light of the Lord's promise, "Ask and you shall receive," such prayer surely is a primary factor in the renewal of the experience of charisms in our day.

There has also been a renewal of certain charisms that were common in the early church but have since become rare and were looked on as extraordinary or even miraculous, such as prophecy, tongues, and healing in answer to prayer. I shall speak at length about these gifts in subsequent chapters.

The attention that has to be given to these somewhat controversial gifts should not make us overlook what to my mind is one of the most important reasons for speaking of a "charismatic renewal"—namely, the renewal that so many have found through participation in it of the fundamental charisms of their lives, such as their vocation to the priesthood or the religious life, or to marriage and parenthood. Indeed, one would have to be suspicious of any claim to have received new charisms, made by a person who showed no sign of a renewed enthusiasm for and commitment to his or her primary charism.

Finally, if we can rightly talk about "charismatic renewal," we have to think in terms not only of the renewal of individuals, but of a charismatic renewal of the church. It seems to me that we have good reasons to judge that this movement is making a real contribution to a charismatic renewal of the Catholic

Church. I see this contribution being made by the influence which groups and communities of this renewal have upon the whole church. I see such groups and communities as a leaven, which gradually has a quickening effect on the whole mass.

I believe that a major role in the charismatic renewal of the church will have to be played by vital Christian communities where the leadership, ministry, and worship are charismatic. I do not claim that it is *only* in the "charismatic renewal" that one can find such communities, but I do say that one can find many of them there. Let us now look at reasons for describing the leadership, ministry, and worship in these communities as charismatic.

Charismatic Leadership

All leadership involves real authority, possessed by one person and recognized by others. The question whether in a particular case leadership is charismatic or formal depends on the source of the authority which the leader possesses, or, in other words, the reason why people recognize the authority of this leader. If the leader's authority comes from the fact that he has been chosen, appointed, ordained to a particular office, the source of his authority is the office which he holds; this is formal authority. Whereas, if his authority comes from the recognition on the part of the community of this person's gift for leadership, this is charismatic authority. Now, of course, it is quite possible for these two sources of authority to be combined in the same person. A person may be chosen for an office because he has already manifested a gift for leadership; or his appointment to an office may provide his first opportunity to exercise his gift for leadership.

It would be ideal if, wherever there is an elected or appointed office in the church, the authority of the office-holder were not only formal but also based on the person's charism for leadership. No doubt this ideal has been realized in many church leaders in the course of history, but it would be unrealistic to claim that this has always been the case. Like any ideal, it is a goal to be aimed at and striven for, and the closer the reality comes to attaining it, the better the condition of the church will be.

When I say that the leadership in groups and communities of the renewal is typically charismatic, I am not claiming any monopoly of charismatic leadership for them, as though there were nothing but formal leadership anywhere else in the church. Nor, on the contrary, do I claim that the leadership in the renewal is purely charismatic, with no admixture of formal authority by reason of office. But I do believe it would be true to say that in the typical group or community of this renewal, the authority of the leaders is based more on the recognition by the group of their charism for leadership than on the fact of their having been given an office to which authority is attached. In other words, if the leaders do have formal authority, they are very likely to have charismatic authority as well.

Charismatic Ministry

Until recently the word "ministry" was normally reserved for the functions that members of the clergy would perform. But the Second Vatican Council confirmed a trend toward a broader understanding of ministry in the church, as, for instance, when it spoke of the duty of pastors "so to shepherd the faithful and recognize their ministries and charisms that all according to their proper roles may cooperate in this common undertaking with one heart."[3]

The word "ministry" is a translation of the Greek word *diakonia,* which is also translated "service." The close association between charisms and ministry in the New Testament is brought out most clearly, perhaps, in 1 Peter 4:10-11: "As each has received a gift [*charisma*] employ it for one another, as good stewards of God's varied grace: whoever speaks, as one who utters oracles of God; whoever renders service [*diakonia*] as one who renders it by the strength which God supplies."

As I see it, the use of the term "charismatic ministry" to

describe the various kinds of services which members of renewal groups perform is justified by the fact that "as each has received a gift, they are employing it for one another, rendering services by the strength which God supplies."

What are the kinds of ministries that one might find operative in a typical prayer group? In answering this question, I shall first speak of ministries that contribute to the building up of the group itself, and then of some which a group might provide for others who do not belong to it.

Ministries within the Group

One of the most effective ministries that goes on in prayer groups is the conducting of Life in the Spirit Seminars. These consist of a series of weekly meetings, involving a talk, discussion, and prayer, designed to help newcomers to reach the best possible disposition with which to ask the Lord to "baptize them in the Spirit." The members of the seminar team, who give the talks and lead the discussions in small groups, are chosen from among the more mature members of the whole prayer group or community. They engage in various kinds of ministry in these seminars: teaching, evangelizing, counselling, exhorting, encouraging, and praying with those who participate. It is my experience that team members who have had no professional training for such ministries very often demonstrate remarkable gifts in performing them.

Most of the ministries which I have just mentioned also contribute to the building up of the group in the regular prayer meetings. There are also various ministries that have to do with sacred scripture, some of which require academic training, and others, such as sharing the fruit of personal prayer and reflection on a passage of the Bible, which do not.

Not surprisingly, much of the ministry of a prayer group will have to do with prayer. Many people will come to the meetings with urgent needs, for which they seek the prayer of the group. There will usually be some time during the meeting set aside for such intercessory prayer. But probably the most effective prayer ministry is carried on after the large meeting is over, when people with special needs are invited to go to a "prayer room," where members of the group who have shown a special gift for helping people by praying with them will pray with them individually.

Ministries to People Outside the Group

Most of the ministries that prayer groups provide would come under the heading of what have traditionally been called "spiritual and corporal works of mercy." One of the most common of these would be various ministries to the sick: visiting them in the hospital or at home, praying with them, and providing for their wants. Many groups are involved in some form of assistance to the poor. One of the best-known examples of this is the "Lord's Food Bank" in Juarez, Mexico, the ministry of a group under the leadership of Fr. Richard Thomas, S.J. Many groups have a ministry to those in prison, visiting them, praying with them, conducting prayer meetings in the jail and helping the prisoners to form their own prayer group, and providing them various kinds of assistance, both spiritual and corporal.

Many observers of the Catholic charismatic renewal have noted that the kinds of social ministry in which its members engage have to do with helping people who are suffering from the ills of society, rather than attacking the ills of society itself. My impression is that this has generally been true of the whole pentecostal movement, and I doubt that it is likely to change very much in the future. Nor do I see this as deplorable, as some observers seem to. To my way of thinking, both healings are needed—the healing of people who are suffering from the ills of society, and the healing of the ills of society itself. But this does not mean that every group must necessarily engage in both of these efforts at healing. It seems to me that each must assess its own capacities, and decide what it is best equipped to do, and on that basis decide what God is calling it to do.

I do not believe that it is in the nature of a prayer group to become a social agitation group, a protest group, or the like. Such groups are formed by people who share the same views not only on the goals to be achieved, but also on the means and methods to be employed in achieving them. A protest group will be made up of people who believe in protest and are ready to engage in it together.

The basis on which prayer groups are formed is very different from this. Of course, the members will share the same Christian ideals and be united in their rejection of injustice and other social evils. But one cannot expect unanimity in such a group as regards specific means and methods to be employed in working to overcome social evils. This is not the basis on which they have come together, and to attempt to impose some specific form of social activism on a group would very likely result in splitting it up.

In my opinion, prayer groups make the right decision when they direct their ministry to the helping of people who are suffering from the ills of society, rather than to the curing of society's ills. This, it seems to me, reflects a sound judgment as to where the group's capacities lie, and therefore is a correct discernment of the charisms of the group as such.

I shall conclude this section by mentioning a kind of ministry to which neo-pentecostal groups certainly are called, and in which it is my hope and expectation that they will engage ever more fully and effectively in the future: I mean the ministry of evangelization, which means the sharing of the message of the gospel with one's neighbor. The power that the disciples received at Pentecost was power to witness to Christ, and therefore a movement that is authentically pentecostal must carry on this witness to the world.

Charismatic Worship

Once again we go back to St. Paul, this time for a description of charismatic worship. The key text here is 1 Corinthians 14:26: "What then, brethren? When you come together, each one has a hymn, a lesson, a revelation, a tongue, or an interpretation. Let all things be done for edification."

In the Pauline communities worship was a function of the whole body of Christ, where each member had a contribution to make, according to the gift which he or she had received. Worship is charismatic when participants are free and are encouraged to exercise whatever gifts they have that will help for edification: that is, for the building up of the community and the expression of its attitudes of praise, worship, petition, and thanksgiving.

The typical prayer group of the Catholic charismatic renewal engages in charismatic worship in two kinds of settings: in the prayer meeting and in the celebration of the Eucharist. Let us look at their worship in each of these settings.

Charismatic Worship in the Prayer Meeting. The first thing that one might notice on entering the place where a prayer meeting is being held is that the people sit in a circle, rather than all facing the same way toward an altar or pulpit. While there will usually be a leader of the meeting, his role will be relatively minor, compared to that of the priest at the Eucharist. The leader will usually speak briefly at the start of the meeting in order to welcome newcomers, to remind everyone of the purpose for which they are gathered, and to encourage all to take an active part. For the benefit of newcomers, he might explain that the meeting will begin with a period of praise and worship, and that prayers of petition are more appropriate in the last part of the meeting. This is typically all the structure that a prayer meeting will have; for the rest of the time each is free to contribute as he or she feels led by the Spirit. Among such contributions St. Paul mentioned "a hymn, a lesson, a revelation, a tongue, or an interpretation." But Paul surely did not intend this to be an exhaustive list of all possible contributions. Let us look first at those which Paul did mention, and then at some others.

—*"A hymn."* The most common way of contributing a hymn in a prayer meeting is to suggest an appropriate song for the group to sing at any particular moment of the meeting.

Another way is simply to begin to sing a hymn, in which the group will join. But sometimes a person with a special gift for music will contribute a new song, of his or her own composition.

—*"A lesson."* The Greek word here is *didache*, which means teaching. For the most part, such teaching is strongly biblical in its inspiration and makes an important contribution to the meeting as a "liturgy of the Word." The teaching may be prepared ahead of time on a chosen theme, or it may be occasioned by a scripture passage that is read during the meeting.

—*"A revelation."* In using this word, St. Paul seems to be referring to one of the functions of the prophet, and, it would seem, to the more extraordinary of these functions (cf. 1 Cor 14:29-30). The more ordinary contribution of the prophet to the meeting would be, in Paul's words, to "speak to men for their upbuilding and encouragement and consolation" (1 Cor 14:3). Earlier in this same letter Paul had referred to both men and women prophesying in the context of public worship (1 Cor 11:4-5). So also, in prayer meetings, a person who receives a word of the Lord for the group is encouraged to share it, and, in doing so, to submit it to the discernment of the group.

—*"A tongue or an interpretation."* Perhaps the most distinctive characteristic of neo-pentecostal prayer groups is their openness to tongues as a gift of the Spirit for prayer and praise. Since I shall devote a chapter to the discussion of this gift, I shall not develop this further now. So let us look at some other gifts that people share in the typical prayer meeting.

Sharing Passages of Scripture. Most of the regular members of prayer groups will be people who read and meditate on a passage of the Bible every day, so it is not unusual that they will come to the meeting with a passage in mind that has been especially meaningful to them during the week. As the occasion offers, they will read such a passage and share their reflections on it with the group.

—*Personal testimony.* One of the most effective ways that people build up the group is by sharing their own experience of coming to know the Lord and the power of his Spirit.

—*Spontaneous prayer*. There are many forms that spontaneous prayer can take during a meeting. In the earlier part of the meeting such prayer will usually be in the form of praise, adoration, and thanksgiving. One person may be moved to speak aloud an extended prayer; or a number of others may offer briefer prayers, sometimes resembling a litany of praise. The reading of a passage of scripture very often will be followed by a person's speaking aloud the prayer that the passage has suggested to him or her. A testimony may stimulate a prayer of thanksgiving for God's grace. The last part of the meeting is usually devoted to prayers of intercession and petition.

Charismatic Worship in the Celebration of the Eucharist. When a prayer group of the charismatic renewal celebrates the Eucharist together, the first part of the Mass—the "Liturgy of the Word"—will usually be characterized by the freedom of all to participate and share their gifts. Of course, the scripture readings that are prescribed or chosen for the Mass will be read with special attention and will usually provide the matter for the homily. But, as time permits, other passages can be read, and reflections shared, by any of the participants.

The penitential rite at the beginning of Mass often develops into a litany of prayers for pardon, with the mention of faults for which people wish to express their repentance. The "Gloria" may be followed by a time of spontaneous singing the praises of God, whether in words or in "tongues." The prayer of the faithful before the offertory will be an especially rich occasion for shared prayer.

During the eucharistic liturgy proper, the role of the celebrant is, of course, primary, but there is a strong sense that all share and exercise the priesthood of Christ in this mystery. The acclamation after the consecration will often develop into a period of "singing in tongues." During the thanksgiving after communion, people are free to express their prayer aloud, for all to share, and this is a time during which a word of prophecy is most likely to be heard.

To conclude: when I speak of the worship that is offered to God in the prayer meetings and eucharistic celebrations of these groups as "charismatic," I mean that each participant is free and is encouraged to share what the Spirit gives him or her to share, to the praise and glory of God and to the building up of the body of Christ. I certainly do not identify the notion "charismatic" with any particular charisms, such as tongues or prophecy, as though one could not have charismatic worship without these, or indeed that these, by themselves, would be enough to guarantee that the worship is genuinely charismatic.

On the other hand, while prophecy and tongues are not essential to charismatic worship, they are certainly characteristic of worship in the charismatic renewal. Along with healings, they tend to raise the most questions in any discussion of the renewal. In the following chapters we shall take a closer look at these somewhat controversial gifts.

SEVEN

Prophecy

WHEN I SPEAK of the charism of prophecy, I intend to distinguish it, on the one hand, from that "sharing in the prophetic office of Christ" which, as Vatican II teaches, characterizes the whole people of God, and, on the other hand, from the prophetic vocation, that is, the calling to be a prophet. To be sure, the prophetic vocation involves the charism of prophecy, but, as we shall see, not everyone who receives the charism of prophesying is called by God to be a prophet.

The second chapter of *Lumen gentium* describes those qualities which belong to the whole church as the people of God. It is not only a priestly people; it is also a prophetic people: "The holy people of God shares also in Christ's prophetic office. It spreads abroad a living witness to Him, especially by means of a life of faith and charity and by offering to God a sacrifice of praise, the tribute of lips which give honor to His name."[1] Another passage of *Lumen gentium* that speaks of this common sharing in the prophetic office of Christ is found in the chapter on the laity. "Christ, the great Prophet, who proclaimed the kingdom of His Father by the testimony of His life and the power of His words, continually fulfills His prophetic office until His full glory is revealed. He does this not only through the hierarchy who teach in His name and with His authority, but also through the laity. For that very purpose He made them His witnesses and gave them understanding of the faith and the grace of speech, so that the power of the gospel might shine forth in their daily social and family life."[2]

Now, it is clear that St. Paul would have agreed that all Christians are called to witness to their faith by word and deed, and in that sense to share in Christ's prophetic office. But on the other hand, Paul speaks of prophecy as one of the charisms, that is, as one of those graces that are distributed among the members of the body of Christ, so that one receives this gift, and another that. For St. Paul, the charism of prophecy is a gift that all Christians should desire to have (cf. 1 Cor 14:1), but it is not something in which all share by the very fact of being Christians.

We have to conclude that when we say that all Christians share in the prophetic office, we are speaking of prophecy as witnessing to one's faith. This is a legitimate use of the term, but this is not what we mean when we talk about the charism of prophecy, which, as a "distributed grace," is given not to all, but to some members for the upbuilding of the the whole body.

I have also said that the charism of prophecy is not to be identified with the vocation to be a prophet, because a person can occasionally receive the charism to prophesy without necessarily being called to be a prophet. This distinction is justified by the way scripture speaks of prophets and prophesying.

For example, in the Old Testament we have the episode of the seventy elders chosen by Moses to help him lead the people (Nm 11:16-30). Of these men it is said: "Then the Lord came down in the cloud and spoke to him [Moses], and took some of the spirit that was upon him and put it upon the seventy elders; and when the spirit rested upon them, they prophesied. But they did so no more" (Nm 11:25). Their prophesying is a sign that God has poured out his spirit upon them; but evidently this did not involve their calling to be prophets.

On the other hand, in the Old Testament we have several accounts of the calling of prophets, which show us what such a vocation entailed. Thus, for example, we read about the calling of Isaiah (Is 6), of Jeremiah (Jer 1), of Ezekiel (Ez 1-3), and of Amos (Amos 7:14-15). In these passages we see that the prophetic vocation involved being sent by God to speak his word to the people. This calling and sending became the dominant factor in the prophet's life. It put him under a constraint to listen for the word of God and, having heard it, to perform actions and proclaim messages that would communicate the divine word to the people. It involved a whole way of life, setting the prophet apart as a man sent by God.

The prophetic vocation did not, of course, mean that the prophet could prophesy whenever he chose. The true prophet could speak only the word that he heard from the Lord. He had to wait for this word and pray to receive it; it was not something under his power to summon up at will.

On the contrary, the sin of the false prophets was that they were prophesying without having been sent by God and without having heard his word. Of such men Jeremiah says, "And the Lord said to me: 'The prophets are prophesying lies in my name; I did not send them, nor did I command them or speak to them. They are prophesying to you a lying vision, worthless divination, and the deceit of their own minds' " (Jer 14:14). Or, as Ezekiel puts it, they are "foolish prophets who follow their own spirit, and have seen nothing! . . . they say, 'Says the Lord,' when the Lord has not sent them, and yet they expect him to fulfill their word" (Ez 13:3-6). Of such prophets God says, "I did not send the prophets, yet they ran; I did not speak to them, yet they prophesied" (Jer 23:21).

In the New Testament the man who most closely resembles the Old Testament prophets is John the Baptist. In the Baptist we see again that the prophetic vocation means being a "man sent by God" (Jn 1:6). John is conscious of his having been sent, and he testifies to it: "He who sent me to baptize with water said to me. . . ." (Jn 1:33-34). We see also in the case of John the Baptist that his prophetic vocation involved a whole way of life, such that he could describe himself simply as "the voice of one crying in the wilderness" (Jn 1:23).

Besides John the Baptist, there are a few others whom the New Testament writers refer to as prophets (Agabus, Judas, and Silas, for instance), but there are many others who prophesy, without their being called prophets, and without any indication that they are marked out by a prophetic vocation. Let us now look more closely at what the New Testament tells us about prophets and prophesying in the early Christian community.

New Testament Prophets

Of the 144 times that the word "prophet" occurs in the New Testament, in no less than 123 cases the reference is to the prophets of the Old Testament. In the other twenty-one instances, the word "prophet" is applied to Jesus, to John the Baptist, and to some members of the Christian community, a few of whom are mentioned by name. Thus, we hear of Agabus (Acts 11:28; 21:10); of five "prophets and teachers" at Antioch, among whom are Barnabas and Saul (Acts 13:1-2); of Judas and Silas (Acts 15:32). Luke also describes the aged widow Anna as a prophetess (Luke 2:36), and tells us that the evangelist Philip had four unmarried daughters who prophesied (Acts 21:9). It is noteworthy that St. Paul, who gives us more information about Christian prophecy than any other New Testament writer, never once mentions any Christian prophet by name.

There are a number of indications that both Paul and Luke consider the men whom they call "prophets" to be important members of the Christian community. We have already seen that on the one occasion when Paul listed the gifts in the order of their importance, he said, "God has appointed in the church first apostles, second prophets, third teachers" (1 Cor 12:28). The letter to the Ephesians describes the church as "built upon the foundation of the apostles and prophets" (Eph 2:20). That Paul has Christian prophets in mind is confirmed by two other passages of the same letter, where he speaks of "apostles and prophets" as those to whom the mystery of the calling of the Gentiles has been revealed (Eph 3:5), and lists the "gifts of Christ to his church" as "apostles, prophets, evangelists, pastors and teachers" (Eph 4:11).

Luke also suggests that prophets had an important role to play in the life of the early church. The five men whom he calls "prophets and teachers" (Acts 13:1-2) were obviously the leaders of the Christian community at Antioch. He also tells us that Judas and Silas, whom he names as prophets (Acts 15:32), were "leading men among the brethren" (Acts 15:22).

While in the letter to the Ephesians the stress is on the prophets' role as mediators of revelation, receiving insight into mysteries and communicating this to the church, the prophets who are mentioned in Acts have a more practical role to play in giving direction to the church. For instance, Agabus predicts a famine, leading the Christians of Antioch to send relief to the churches of Judea (Acts 11:27-30). The five who are called prophets and teachers at Antioch make the decision, guided by prophecy, that Saul and Barnabas should set out on a missionary journey, and "after fasting and praying they laid hands on them and sent them off" (Acts 13:1-3). Judas and Silas are chosen to communicate the decisions taken at Jerusalem to the church at Antioch (Acts 15:22-34).

"Congregational Prophecy"

J. Reiling[3] has coined this phrase to describe the prophesying that was done by members of the early Christian communities who were not given the title "prophets," and who did not have the leading role in the community that those called prophets had. There are a number of indications that such prophesying, by people who were not among the recognized "prophets," was a common phenomenon in the New Testament church.

First of all, we can conclude from Acts 2:16ff. that the early Christians saw in their own experience the fulfillment of the prophecy of Joel about the "last days": "And in the last days it shall be, God declares, that I will pour out my Spirit upon all flesh, and your sons and your daughters shall prophesy, and your young men shall see visions, and your old men shall dream dreams; yea, and on my menservants and my maidservants in those days I will pour out my Spirit; and they shall prophesy" (Jl 3:1-2). In the Old Testament the Spirit of God was most typically understood as the spirit of prophecy, which was poured out not on all the people, but on those individuals whom

God called to speak his word. So strong was the association between the Spirit and prophecy in the Jewish mind, that it led to the idea that when there were no longer any prophets, the Holy Spirit was no longer present. Thus one finds in rabbinic writings the saying, "Since the death of the last prophets, Haggai, Zechariah and Malachi, the Holy Spirit departed from Israel."[4]

The early Christians could hardly have made the claim that this prophecy of Joel was already being fulfilled, unless they had the experience of such an abundant outpouring of the gift of prophecy in the Christian community that both men and women, young and old, were heard to prophesy. A number of passages in Acts and the letters of Paul bear out this hypothesis.

In Acts 19:6 Luke tells us that when Paul baptized the twelve who had been disciples of John the Baptist and laid his hands on them, "The Holy Spirit came on them; and they spoke with tongues and prophesied." There is no indication that these men were subsequently known as prophets.

During St. Paul's last journey to Jerusalem, Luke has him say, "The Holy Spirit testifies to me in every city that imprisonment and afflictions await me" (Acts 20:23). That what "the Holy Spirit testifies to" is spoken in prophecy is confirmed by the formula used by Agabus in prophesying: "Thus says the Holy Spirit" (Acts 21:11). We can conclude that this warning was given to Paul through prophecy in every Christian community he had visited on this journey. We have an indication that Luke does not restrict such prophesying to recognized prophets in the way he speaks of this same warning as given to Paul in Tyre. He tells us that when they arrived at Tyre, "having sought out the disciples, we stayed there for seven days. Through the Spirit they told Paul not to go on to Jerusalem" (Acts 21:4). The formula "through the Spirit" marks this warning as given in prophecy, but Luke attributes it to "the disciples," without specifying that those who spoke it were prophets.

The earliest reference to prophecy in the letters of Paul is found in 1 Thessalonians 5:19-21: "Do not quench the Spirit, do not despise prophesying, but test everything; hold fast to what is good." From this we know beyond doubt that some members of this community were prophesying. No mention, however, is made of prophets, even though a few verses earlier Paul had spoken of those who "labored among" them and "were over" them and "admonished them" (1 Thes 5:12).

The first reference to prophecy in 1 Corinthians strongly suggests that Paul is speaking of "congregational prophecy." What is at issue in the passage is the question whether the Corinthians ought to observe the tradition of the Judaeo-Christian communities regarding the headgear to be worn while actively participating in liturgical worship (1 Cor 11:2-16). Paul strongly urges the observance of this tradition: "Any man who prays or prophesies with his head covered dishonours his head, but any woman who prays or prophesies with her head unveiled dishonours her head—it is the same as if her head were shaven" (1 Cor 11:4-5). From the way Paul speaks here of men and women praying and prophesying, one certainly gets the impression that he expected others to prophesy besides "prophets," whom he named second to the apostles among those whom "God has appointed in the church" (1 Cor 12:28).

This impression is confirmed by Paul's discussion of prophecy in 1 Corinthians 14. In the very first verse of this chapter, Paul exhorts the Corinthians to "earnestly desire the spiritual gifts, especially that you may prophesy." It hardly seems likely that Paul meant that they should all aspire to be prophets. But the exhortation makes good sense if Paul is thinking of the inspiration to prophesy that any member of the congregation might on occasion receive, as his or her contribution to the common worship. So Paul could say, a few verses further on, "Now I want you all to speak in tongues, but even more to prophesy" (14:5). Of course this does not mean that Paul expected everyone actually to prophesy, any more than he expected everyone to speak in tongues. This would contradict the sense of his question in 12:30: "Do all speak in tongues?" Paul's wish that all might speak in tongues and prophesy is simply a way of expressing his esteem for these gifts, just as his wish that all might be celibate as he himself was (1 Cor 7:7) is a way of expressing his esteem for this gift, without implying that he really expected all to have it.

But, someone might ask, does not Paul speak of the effect it would have on an unbeliever if he should come into the assembly when "all are prophesying" (14:24)? And does he not say, a few verses further on, "For you can all prophesy, one by one, so that all may learn and all be encouraged" (14:31)?

To my mind these verses do confirm the view that Paul expected others besides recognized prophets to receive the charism of prophesying in the assembly. But I doubt that one should interpret him to mean that literally all would prophesy. In verse 24 the case is explicitly hypothetical, and almost certainly hyperbolic as well. With regard to verse 31, I think it more probable that the phrase "You can all prophesy one by one" means "All of you who receive the charism of prophecy can exercise this gift, but you must await your turn." No one is excluded from the possibility of receiving a charism to prophesy, or from exercising the gift if he or she receives it, but that does not mean that literally everyone will prophesy.

While I think it unwarranted to conclude from 1 Corinthians 14:24, 31 that Paul really expected everyone in the Christian community to prophesy, his discussion of prophecy in this chapter certainly confirms the impression that he knew and encouraged congregational prophecy. He closes this chapter as he began it, by telling the Corinthians that they should earnestly desire to prophesy. It is hard to imagine what such an exhortation could mean except that they should be as open as possible to receiving an inspiration to prophesy, as their contribution to the common liturgy.

The Function of Prophecy in the Christian Community

In this section we are going to look at what the New Testament writers tell us about the usefulness of the gift of prophecy, or, in other words, about the contribution which those who prophesy make to the life of the community. In talking about "those who prophesy," we include both those whose vocation it is to be prophets, and those who occasionally prophesy.

If we compare what Paul and Luke tell us about the function of prophecy in the Christian community, we find some points of similarity and some of contrast. Whereas Luke stresses the notion of prophecy as prediction of future events, by which people can be guided in decisions they have to make, Paul nowhere mentions the predicting of the future as part of the prophet's role. On the other hand, there is a striking agreement between Luke and Paul in their use of the verb *parakalein* and the cognate noun *paraklesis* to describe the function of prophecy.

It is difficult to translate the verb *parakalein* by just one English word, because it can mean to encourage, to exhort, or to console. Likewise the noun *paraklesis* can mean encouragement, exhortation, or consolation. In the following passages, the words *exhort* and *encourage* translate *parakalein,* and the words *exhortation* and *encouragement* translate *paraklesis.*

Luke's summary description of the preaching of the prophet John the Baptist is as follows: "So, with many other *exhortations,* he preached good news to the people (Lk 3:18). Luke translates the Aramaic name Barnabas, which the Apostles conferred on the disciple Joseph, as "Son of encouragement" (Acts 4:36, RSV), thus indicating what his function was in the community. When news of the conversion of Gentiles at Antioch "came to the ears of the church at Jerusalem, they sent Barnabas to Antioch. When he came and saw the grace of God, he was glad; and he *exhorted* them all to remain faithful to the Lord with steadfast purpose, for he was a good man, full of the Holy Spirit and of faith" (Acts 11:22-24). A little while later, Luke names Barnabas in first place among the "prophets and teachers" at Antioch (13:1).

The passage in Acts that most clearly brings out the idea that a prophet's role is to exhort and to encourage, is found in 15:32—"And Judas and Silas, who were themselves prophets, *exhorted* the brethren with many words and strengthened them." The parenthetical phrase "who were themselves prophets" makes it clear that this is the kind of speech that the early Christians would expect to hear from a prophet, and the kind of effect they would expect his words to have.

The place where St. Paul has spoken in greatest detail about prophecy is in chapter 14 of 1 Corinthians. Of course we should not imagine that he intended to give us a treatise on prophecy that would answer all our questions. He was writing to people who knew what prophecy was, but who did not hold it in the esteem that it deserved, preferring the more spectacular gift of speaking in tongues. What Paul says about prophecy was intended to convince the Corinthians that it is superior to glossolalia, rather than to explain what it is.

Fortunately for us, however, 1 Corinthians 14 still does shed considerable light on Paul's understanding of the function of prophecy. In particular, there are two verses which describe the effects which he expected prophecy to have on the gathered community. Verse 3 reads: "He who prophesies speaks to men for their upbuilding and encouragement and consolation." Verse 31 reads: "For you can all prophesy one by one, so that all may learn and all be encouraged." Here we see that when Paul spoke of the usefulness of prophecy, he described its function as "encouragement" (*paraklesis*). The other uses he mentions are also instructive: for "upbuilding," and "consolation," and so that "all may learn."

Prophecy is clearly different from, and superior to, glossolalia, in that it is intelligible speech, by which people are "built up" and can "learn." However, it is not so immediately evident how prophecy differs from the gifts of preaching and teaching. I think to grasp this difference we have to fall back on the basic premise of the whole chapter, namely, that prophecy, for Paul as well as for the Corinthians, was a prime example of the *pneumatika,* the gifts of inspiration. We see this in the very first verse of the chapter, when Paul urges the Corinthians to "earnestly desire the *pneumatika,* especially that you may prophesy." I fully agree with Dunn when he says, "[Paul] contrasts prophecy and glossolalia not as to inspiration, but as to intelligibility: prophecy is as much inspired speech, as much 'speaking with the Spirit,' as much a charisma, as glossolalia; the difference is that glossolalia is unintelligible whereas prophecy is intelligible. . . . In short, *prophecy in Paul cannot denote anything other than inspired speech.*"[5]

The essential difference, then, between prophecy and any other kind of speaking by which the community can be built up is the element of inspiration that is proper to prophetic speech. In other words, the preacher or teacher has a habitual gift, which he can use at will; the prophet can only prophesy when he is inspired to do so; that is, when he has a message to communicate that he is convinced he has received from God. As we have seen earlier, this seems to be the correct interpretation of Paul's phrase, "prophecy, in proportion to one's faith" (Rom 12:6), where "faith" is the assurance that one is being genuinely inspired to speak.

Another indication of the difference between prophecy and other kinds of speech that could build up the community is the close association which Paul makes between prophecy and revelation. We see this most clearly in 1 Corinthians 14:29-30: "Let two or three prophets speak, and let the others weigh what is said. If a revelation is made to another sitting by, let the first be silent." This suggests that while not every prophecy is a revelation, at least some prophecies are, and that prophecies that are revelations take precedence over those which are not.

A rather puzzling statement which Paul makes to show the superiority of prophecy over glossolalia is that whereas "tongues are a sign not for believers but for unbelievers, prophecy is not for unbelievers but for believers" (1 Cor 14:22). The problem is that it is not immediately clear in what sense Paul is using the expression "to be a sign for." I suggest that we first look at the sense of his whole argument here, and then come back to try to determine the meaning of verse 22.

What Paul is doing in this section (vv. 20-25) is showing the superiority of prophecy over tongues by comparing the effects which the exercise of these gifts would have on an unbeliever who might come into the Christian assembly. Tongues would only serve to confirm the unbeliever in his unbelief, whereas prophecy would move him from unbelief to belief. Each of the gifts, then, is being described as "a sign of" what *results* from its exercise. Speaking in tongues makes people (is a sign for) unbelievers; prophecy makes them (is a sign for) believers.

If we ask how prophecy brings the unbeliever to belief, we see that it does this by bringing him to a conviction of his own sinfulness and to the recognition of the presence of God in the Christian community that reveals his sinfulness to him. One need not take the phrase "the secrets of his heart are disclosed" to mean public disclosure of his secret sins. It more probably means that his eyes are opened to his own sinfulness, so that he judges himself a sinner in need of God's mercy. This would be another instance of prophecy that has the function of revelation, as well as the specific function of convicting the sinner and calling him to account, so as to bring him to repentance and faith.

Having seen how St. Paul describes the "useful purpose" which prophecy serves in the Christian community, let us now look at some other references to prophecy in the New Testament to see what further light they shed on this question.

In 1 Timothy we find two mentions of prophecy, both in reference to prophecies which evidently had indicated the ministry for which Timothy was to be ordained (1 Tm 1:18 and 4:14). We are reminded of Acts 13:2, where "the Holy Spirit said: 'Set apart for me Barnabas and Saul for the work to which I have called them.'" So we have in 1 Timothy another example of the kind of prophecy that guided the leaders of the church in making practical decisions, a kind that revealed God's intentions regarding the role that certain persons were to have in the ministry.

To conclude this section we should take a look at what are no doubt the best examples of Christian prophecies that the New Testament has preserved for us: namely, the seven "letters to the churches" in Revelation 2-3. There is every indication that the author presents these "letters" as prophecies. First of all, in Revelation 1:10-11 he says, "I was in the Spirit on the Lord's day, and I heard behind me a loud voice like a trumpet saying, 'Write what you see in a book and send it to the seven churches.' " The phrase "to be in the Spirit," which occurs several times in this book (e.g., 4:2; 17:3), is undoubtedly equivalent to being "under inspiration," a state in which he "hears" and "sees" what God wishes him to communicate. The "one like a son of man" who appears to him and speaks to him (1:12-13) is the risen Christ, who says to him, "Now write what you see, what is and what is to take place hereafter" (1:19).

Each of the seven letters which follow is presented, with a different formula each time, as the words of the glorious Christ (see 2:1, 8, 12, 18; 3:1, 7, 14). Thus they follow the pattern of Old Testament prophecies, which present themselves as the "word of the Lord." And each of the seven letters concludes with the admonition: "He who has an ear, let him hear what the Spirit says to the churches" (2:7, 11, 17, 29; 3:6, 13, 22). The writer could hardly have made it clearer that what he is communicating is not his own word but the word of the risen Lord, received through the Spirit, in other words, prophecy.

When one examines the contents of the seven letters, one sees how remarkably they conform to St. Paul's idea of the function of prophecy: "The prophet speaks to men for their upbuilding and encouragement and consolation" (1 Cor 14:3). We see here, too, as elsewhere, that "upbuilding and encouragement" can also involve words of stern rebuke and admonition when this is needed. One of the functions of prophecy, as we have seen, is to bring sinners to a conviction of their sinfulness and need of repentance. This is especially to be seen in the letters to the churches in Sardis (3:1-6) and Laodicea (3:14-22).

False Prophets in the Christian Community

It is clear from both the Old and the New Testament that the acceptance of prophecy as a gift from God to the community involves the necessity of discernment between true and false prophecy. It seems inevitable that a community that is disposed to accept certain persons as prophets and their utterances as inspired by God is going to have to contend with the problem of false prophets as well. There is no need to dwell here on the Old Testament experience, of which we have spoken briefly already. Let us look at what the New Testament tells us about false prophets in the Christian community.

There is good reason to judge that the problem posed by false prophets was felt particularly keenly by the community for which the Gospel of Matthew was written. This is the only Gospel which gives us Jesus' warning against the false prophets who will come among his followers: "Beware of false prophets, who come to you in sheep's clothing but inwardly are ravenous wolves" (Mt 7:15). There can be little doubt that the "sheep's clothing" refers to their profession of Christian faith and fellowship. This is confirmed by the plea which such false prophets will make on the day of judgment: "Lord, Lord, did we not prophesy in your name, and cast out demons in your name, and do many mighty works in your name?" (Mt 7:22). If we look at the parallel passages in the Gospel of Luke, we see that what in Luke is a generic teaching about the punishment in store for evildoers, in Matthew is specifically applied to false prophets (c.p. Lk 6:43-46 and 13:26-27). The most probable explanation of this is that Matthew's community was experiencing the harm that such false prophets were doing to the church.

There are two other mentions of false prophets in Matthew's Gospel, both referring to the appearance of many false prophets as one of the tribulations of the "last days" (Mt 24:11, 24). It is noteworthy that here again it is taken for granted that even false prophets can "show great signs and wonders," just as in 7:22 they could claim to have "done many mighty works" in the name of Christ. This suggests that perhaps Matthew's community had experienced wonder-working prophets who turned out to be "wolves in sheep's clothing." In any case, it shows an awareness that the ability to work signs and wonders is not sufficient proof that a prophet is genuine.

The First Letter of John also speaks of false prophets as a problem with which the Christian community had to contend

(1 Jn 4:1-3): "Beloved, do not believe every spirit, but test the spirits to see whether they are of God; for many false prophets have gone out into the world." Finally, in the Book of Revelation, the letter to the church in Thyatira speaks of "the woman Jezebel who calls herself a prophetess and is teaching and beguiling my servants to practice immorality and to eat food sacrificed to idols" (Rv 2:20).

The "Discernment of Spirits"

I have already expressed my opinion in agreement with the consensus of New Testament scholars that the "ability to distinguish between spirits," which Paul lists among the charisms in 1 Corinthians 12:10, is primarily concerned with the gift immediately preceding it in the same list, namely, prophecy. Prophecy is inspired speech, and "distinguishing between spirits" has to do with determining by what spirit the speaker is inspired. Dunn suggests that in the term "discernment of spirits" (*diakrisis pneumaton*) the word *pneumata* can be understood as equivalent to *pneumatika*, in which case it can be translated by "inspirations" or "inspired utterances." Thus, he proposes to translate *diakrisis pneumaton* as "an evaluation, an investigating, a testing, a weighing of the prophetic utterance by the rest [of the assembly or of the prophets] to determine both its source as to inspiration and its significance for the assembly."[6] This interpretation is supported by Paul's directive in 1 Corinthians 14:29, where again the gifts of prophecy and discernment are put in close association: "Let two or three prophets speak, and let the others weigh what is said" (the Greek word translated "weigh" is a verbal form of *diakrisis*). Likewise, in 1 Thessalonians 5:19-22 we see that prophecy calls for testing and discernment of what is good: "Do not quench the Spirit, do not despise prophesying, but test everything; hold fast to what is good, abstain from every form of evil."

Let us look now at the criteria by which such discernment is to be made. We have already seen in Matthew 7:22-23 that the ability to work signs and wonders, to cast out demons and do mighty works in the name of Jesus, is no conclusive proof of a true prophet. Even the false prophet and evildoer can accomplish such things.

The New Testament writers suggest two criteria for distinguishing between true and false prophets: the moral uprightness of the prophet, and the orthodoxy of his prophecies. We have already seen that in Matthew, the false prophets are to be recognized by the "bad fruit" which they bear. At the last judgment they will be denounced as "evildoers." Their description as "ravenous wolves who come in sheep's clothing" suggests that the bad fruit which they bear can be understood as the harm which they do to the Christian communities in which they exercise their pretended gift of prophecy.

Similarly the false prophetess Jezebel is denounced for her immorality, of which she refuses to repent, and into which she leads other "servants of the Lord" (Rv 2:20, 21).

Orthodoxy of teaching about Jesus is the criterion which the First Letter of John proposes for discerning between the true and the false prophet: "By this you know the Spirit of God: every spirit which confesses that Jesus Christ has come in the flesh is of God, and every spirit which does not confess Jesus is not of God" (1 Jn 4:2-3). For St. Paul also, what a person says under inspiration about Jesus shows by what kind of spirit the speaker is inspired (1 Cor 12:3).

There are two passages in early Christian, but non-canonical writings, which treat the question of the criteria by which true prophets can be distinguished from false. They are the 11th chapter of *The Didache*, and the 11th Mandate in *The Shepherd of Hermas*. In both passages, the emphasis is on the prophet's way of life, rather than on the orthodoxy of his teaching. Thus, *The Didache* warns: "Not everyone who speaks forth in the spirit is a prophet, but only if he has the kind of behavior which the Lord approves. From his behavior, then, will the false prophet and the true prophet be known. And every prophet who, in the spirit, orders a table to be spread shall not eat therefrom, but if he does, he is a false prophet. And every prophet who teaches the truth, but does not do the things he teaches, is a false prophet."[7] Presumably, one who does not teach the truth would also be recognized thereby as a false prophet, but what the author of *The Didache* wishes to stress is that the truth of the prophet's teaching is not a sufficient criterion of the true prophet; he must also live up to his teaching.

The prophet's manner of life is again the criterion proposed in the 11th Mandate of *The Shepherd of Hermas.* While the passage is rather long, it seems worth quoting since it is the most interesting discussion of the gift of prophecy that we find in early Christian literature.

7. "Sir," I said, "how then will a man know which of them is a prophet and which is a false prophet?" "Hear," he said, "about both prophets, and in the manner that I am going to tell you, you can test the prophet and the false prophet. By his life you test the man that has the divine Spirit.

8. First, then, the one who has the Spirit from above is gentle and quiet and humble, and refrains from all evil and worthless desires of this age, and makes himself more needy than all other men, and when asked, gives no answer to anyone. Neither does he speak by himself, nor does the holy Spirit speak whenever a man wishes to speak, but he speaks when God wishes him to speak.

9. So whenever the man who has the divine Spirit comes into an assembly of righteous men who have faith in the divine Spirit, and a prayer is made to God by the assembly of these men, then the angel of the prophetic gift which is assigned to him fills the man, and that man, having been filled by the holy Spirit, speaks to the group as the Lord wills.

10. So in this way the divine Spirit is known. So whatever power pertains to the spirit of deity is of the Lord.

11. Hear now," he said, "about the spirit which is earthly and empty and has no power, but is foolish.

12. In the first place, that man who thinks he has the spirit elevates himself and wishes to have a seat of honor, and right away he is bold and shameless and talkative, and lives in great

luxury and in many other pleasures, and accepts pay for his prophesying. And if he does not receive, he does not prophesy. Is it possible, then, for a divine Spirit to accept a salary for prophesying? It is not possible for a prophet of God to do this, but the spirit of such prophets is earthly.

13. Next, he never comes near an assembly of righteous men, but shuns them. But he associates with the double minded and the empty, and prophesies to them in a corner, and he deceives them by saying everything in an empty manner, according to their desires, for he is answering those who are empty. For that empty vessel which is placed with others that are empty is not broken, but they harmonize with one another.

14. But whenever he comes into an assembly full of righteous men who have the divine Spirit and prayer is offered by them, that man is emptied, and the earthly spirit flees from him in fear, and that man is rendered speechless and is completely shattered, being unable to say a thing. . . .

16. You have before you the life of both kinds of prophets. By his deeds and life, then, test the man who says he is inspired."[8]

It is noteworthy that both *The Didache* and *The Shepherd of Hermas* provide practical norms for the discernment of the true from the false prophet, rather than for the discernment of true from false prophecies. Their approach seems to be: look to the reliability of the prophet, and when you are satisfied that he is genuine, you can accept his prophecies without fear of being deceived.

The Charism of Prophecy in the Early Church

Since our discussion of the criteria for distinguishing between true and false prophets has led us to consult early non-canonical Christian writings, let us now look briefly at the evidence for the continuing experience of the charism of prophecy in the Christian church of the first two centuries.

First of all, the passage we have already quoted from *The Didache* shows that at the period at which this was written (late first century, in the more common view), prophets were highly respected members of the Christian community. There was a delicate balance to be observed in the relationship between community and prophet: the community had the right to pass judgment (in the light of his conduct) as to whether a man who claimed prophetic gifts was indeed a true prophet or not; but once it was clear that he was a true prophet, they were not to judge his prophecies or his prophetic actions: "And you must neither make trial nor pass judgment on any prophet who speaks forth in the spirit. For every other sin will be forgiven, but this sin will not be forgiven. . . . And every prophet who has met the test—who is genuine—and who performs a worldly mystery of the church but does not teach others to do what he is doing, he shall not be judged by you. For he has his judgment with God—for the ancient prophets also did similarly."[9]

Other references to prophets in *The Didache* bring out further aspects of their role in the Christian community of that period. At the conclusion of the prayer to be used in the celebration of the Eucharist, *The Didache* adds, "But permit the prophets to give thanks as they see fit,"[10] suggesting that the prophets had a special role in the community's liturgy. This idea is further strengthened when we read the prescriptions for the material support of the prophets who take up residence in a Christian community: "And every prophet who wishes to settle among you deserves his food. Similarly, a true teacher also deserves, like the laborer, his food. Take, therefore, every first fruit—of the produce of wine press and threshing floor, and of cattle and sheep—and give it to the prophets. For they are your high priests. But if you have no prophet, give to the poor."[11] This last remark suggests that a Christian community might not have a resident prophet. What should be done in this case is indicated later on: "Appoint for yourselves, then, bishops and deacons who are worthy of the Lord—men who are unassuming and not greedy, who are honest and have been proved. For they also are performing for you the task of the prophets and teachers.

Therefore do not hold them in contempt, for they are honorable men among you, along with the prophets and teachers."[12]

This is not the place to enter into a discussion of the many questions which this fascinating document raises about the development of ministry in the early church. It does seem to reflect a time of transition, when the position of prophets and teachers was already well established, whereas that of bishops and deacons still needed to be strengthened in the eyes of the Christian community. Another interesting point is that while we find ample evidence in *The Didache* of the presence of recognized prophets, with a distinct role in the community's life and worship, we do not find any reference to congregational prophecy, that is, to the gift of prophesying which any man or woman in the Christian assembly might occasionally receive.

On the other hand, the passage which we have already quoted from *The Shepherd of Hermas* has been seen by a scholar who has made an exhaustive study of this passage, as evidence of the practice of congregational prophecy in the Roman church toward the middle of the second century. J. Reiling sees it as particularly significant that in Mandate 11, verse 9, Hermas does not use the title "prophet," but speaks more generically of "the man who has the divine Spirit."

In this crucial passage the word *prophetes* is conspicuously absent. Instead, the Shepherd refers to the prophet as "the man who has the divine Spirit." His endowment with the Spirit is not different from that of his fellow believers with whom he is gathered in the congregation. He is not a *pneumatikos* over against a congregation which is endowed with the Spirit in a lesser degree. It is the false prophet who alleges that he is a *pneumatophoros* [Spirit-bearer] and thereby discredits himself by this very allegation. When, however, the congregation and the prophet have the same endowment with the divine Spirit, then it certainly follows that any member of the congregation can be chosen by the Spirit to be filled and to speak as the Lord wills. The church consists of potential prophets. There is no specific prophetic order within the church, but the church itself is a prophetic order. . . . The 11th Mandate is unequivocal evidence that prophecy as a congregational *charisma* is found in the second century A.D.[13]

Reiling also stresses Hermas' idea of the dependence of the prophet on the Spirit in the gathered congregation; it is in answer to the prayer of the "assembly of righteous men" that the Spirit inspires one of their number to speak in prophecy. As Reiling sums up the evidence from the 11th Mandate: "To sum up, in Hermas' understanding and experience, the Holy Spirit—which the believers received in their baptism and which changed their lives from death to life—forges them into the one body of the church. The Spirit is present and active in their daily life, and prepares them for the eschatological consummation. This daily life in the Spirit makes the believers fit to be filled with the Spirit when they meet and pray together. When this happens, one of them becomes a prophet and speaks to his fellow-believers as the Lord wants him to speak."[14]

Reiling also sees evidence of the continuing experience of congregational prophecy during the second century in remarks made by two other Christian writers of this period: St. Justin Martyr, and St. Irenaeus, Bishop of Lyons. Let us look briefly at what these two authors tell us about prophecy in the second-century Christian community.

In his *Dialogue with Trypho,* Justin advances an argument for the truth of Christianity against the claims of his Jewish opponent, on the grounds that whereas the gift of prophecy was no longer found among the Jewish people, it was common among Christians. He argues, "From the fact that even to this day the gifts of prophecy exist among us Christians, you should realize that the gifts which had resided among your people have now been transferred to us."[15] Reiling sees in the fact that Justin does not mention any contemporary Christian prophets by name, an indication that it was congregational prophecy that he had in mind.[16]

Similarly, St. Irenaeus speaks in several places of prophecy and prophetic charisms as matters of experience in the church of his day. Because the testimony of Irenaeus to the experience of prophecy and other charisms in the church toward the end of the second century is so pertinent to our subject, it seems worthwhile to quote him even at some length.

In a passage where Irenaeus had been speaking of the miracles of Jesus, he continues:

> Wherefore also, those who are in truth his disciples, receiving grace from him, do works in his name, so as to promote the welfare of other men, according to the gifts which each one has received from him. For some do certainly and truly drive out devils, so that those who have thus been cleansed from evil spirits frequently both believe and join themselves to the church. Others have foreknowledge of things to come: they see visions and utter prophetic expressions. Others still heal the sick by laying their hands upon them and they are made whole. Yea, moreover, as I have said, the dead even have been raised up, and remained among us for many years. And what more shall I say? It is not possible to name the number of the gifts which the church, throughout the whole world, has received from God, in the name of Jesus Christ, who was crucified under Pontius Pilate, and which she exerts day by day for the benefit of the Gentiles, neither practising deception upon any, nor taking any reward from them. For as she has received freely from God, freely also does she minister to others.[17]

In another passage we see that for Irenaeus, prophecy was an abiding gift to the church, a fruit of Christ's promise to send the Paraclete. He is arguing against heretics who denied this.

> Others again, that they may set at naught the gift of the Spirit, which in the latter times has been by the good pleasure of the Father, poured out upon the human race, do not admit that aspect presented by John's Gospel, in which the Lord promised that he would send the Paraclete; but set aside at

once both the Gospel and the prophetic Spirit. Wretched men indeed! who wish to be pseudo-prophets, forsooth, but who set aside the gift of prophecy from the church; acting like those who, on account of such as come in hypocrisy, hold themselves aloof from the communion of the brethren. We must conclude, moreover, that these men cannot admit the Apostle Paul either. For, in his Epistle to the Corinthians, he speaks expressly of prophetical gifts, and recognizes men and women prophesying in the church. Sinning, therefore, in all these particulars, against the Spirit of God, they fall into the irremissible sin.[18]

The comparison which Irenaeus makes in this passage between the heretics who reject the gift of prophecy, and those who, "on account of such as come in hypocrisy, hold themselves aloof from the communion of the brethren," suggests that his opponents were using the danger of false prophets in the church as a pretext for their utter rejection of the gift of prophecy. The reply of Irenaeus is that just as the presence of some hypocrites in the church does not justify withdrawal from the communion of the brethren, neither does the presence of false prophets justify the rejection of prophecy as such. It is also noteworthy that Irenaeus refers to the passage of 1 Corinthians where St. Paul speaks most clearly of "congregational prophecy" (1 Cor 11:4-5), and in a way that suggests that Irenaeus was familiar with such prophesying by both men and women in the church of his own day. It is obvious that Irenaeus did not think that such prophesying should have ceased at the close of the apostolic age; rather he saw it as a sign of the continued presence of the Holy Spirit in the church.

Indeed, there is good evidence that Irenaeus was expressing the common opinion of Christians of his day, when he insisted that prophecy should continue to be an element in the life of the church. One proof of this is found in a quotation which the church historian Eusebius makes from a third-century writing against the Montanists.[19] Evidently, when this work was written, Montanus and his first disciples, including the prophetess Maximilla, were dead; the argument, directed to the second generation of Montanists, runs as follows:

> For, if the Montanist woman received the prophetic gift after Quadratus and Amnia in Philadelphia, let them show who among them succeeded the followers of Montanus and the women; for the Apostle held that the gift of prophecy must exist in all the church until the final coming. But they would not be able to show this anywhere today, the fourteenth year after the death of Maximilla.[20]

For this unknown Christian writer, the failure of the Montanists to produce any more prophets after the death of Maximilla is proof that they are not the true church, since "the gift of prophecy must exist in all the church until the final coming." Most likely, if asked for proof of this statement, the writer would have appealed to the words of St. Paul: "For our knowledge is imperfect and our prophecy is imperfect; but when the perfect comes, the imperfect will pass away" (1 Cor 13:9-10).

However, it does seem true that the third century did see a decline in the experience of prophecy in the church.[21] Opinions vary as to the degree to which the reaction to the excesses of Montanism had the effect of discouraging the exercise of the genuine charism of prophecy in the churches. Very likely this had something to do with it, although it is hardly the only factor involved. But one reason that has been alleged for the decline of prophecy is quite certainly not the true cause: namely, the argument that once the apostolic age of revelation was over, there could be no more prophecy in the church. There is no evidence that such an opinion was held by Christian writers of the third century, or that such reasoning was made the basis for an exclusion of prophecy, on principle, from the ongoing life of the church. In fact, while the third century saw a decline in the practice of congregational prophecy, there was not then, nor has there been since, an exclusion on principle, or complete lack, of the charism of prophecy in the Catholic Church. As George Montague has put it:

Prophecy, as it had been known at Corinth, was no longer considered proper for the sanctuary. . . . It did not, however, wholly die. It went instead to the arena with the martyrs, to the desert with the fathers, to the monasteries with Benedict, to the streets with Francis, to the cloisters with Teresa of Avila and John of the Cross, to the heathen with Francis Xavier. The passion felt at Corinth to share the experience of the Lord found expression in freely and privately associated groups, in religious orders and confraternities, which were eventually either condemned or approved by the Church. And without bearing the name of prophets, charismatics like Joan of Arc and Catherine of Siena would have a profound influence on the public life of *polis* and Church.[22]

The full history of the charism of prophecy in the Christian era still remains to be written. Some studies have been done, and no doubt others will be undertaken.[23] It is not my intention here to attempt to make even a modest contribution to such a history of prophecy. Instead, I shall limit myself, in the rest of this chapter, to some remarks about prophecy in the charismatic renewal.

Prophecy in the Charismatic Renewal

I think that inevitably one's judgment about prophecy in the charismatic renewal is going to be influenced by one's prior judgment about the likelihood that a genuine gift of congregational prophecy could become again, in our time, as common a gift in Christian communities as it was in St. Paul's day. Any a priori judgment that excludes this hypothesis would of course necessitate the conclusion that people in the charismatic renewal are deluded in taking what they are experiencing to be genuine gifts of prophecy. Personally, I see no justification for such an a priori judgment.

As we have seen, St. Paul exhorted the Corinthians "earnestly to desire the gift of prophecy," since this was a most useful gift for building up the community. If this gift really is as useful to a Christian community as St. Paul evidently judged it to be, and is something which even ordinary Christians should "earnestly desire to have," I see no reason to reject outright the possibility that the Holy Spirit might be giving this gift today to ordinary Christians who earnestly desire it, and ask for it, for the sake of its usefulness for the building up of their communities.

If I am not mistaken, one reason for the scepticism of many about the gifts of prophecy that are claimed in the renewal is the assumption that prophecy must be a rather extraordinary gift of the Spirit. Again, if I am not mistaken, the reason for this is that prophecy has been so commonly understood to mean the ability to predict the future, or to reveal things that only God could know. Now it is true, of course, that we do find some examples of predictive prophecies in the New Testament, especially in Acts. But it is noteworthy that St. Paul nowhere speaks of predictive prophecy. He speaks only of the kind of prophecy that is useful for the "upbuilding, encouragement and con- solation" of the church; the kind of prophecy from which "all may learn and all may be encouraged" (1 Cor 14:3, 31). As we have seen, Paul was familiar with congregational prophecy, that is, the occasional gift by which any man or woman in the congregation might be inspired to speak the word that the Lord wanted the church to hear. Such a word did not have to be, and in most cases probably was not, a prediction about the future or a revelation of something otherwise hidden. It was most typically a word of *paraklesis,* which could mean encourage- ment, admonition, rebuke, warning, consolation. What made such words of *paraklesis* different from any other kind of preaching was that they came across to the community with an effectiveness, a power, that marked them out as more than merely human exhortation. They were recognized as in some real sense the word of the Lord: the word that the Lord wanted the group, or perhaps some particular members of the group, to hear and take to heart. I think that there are good reasons for judging that in a good many instances, what is being recognized as prophecy in prayer groups of the charismatic renewal is the same kind of gift of which St. Paul was speaking in 1 Corinthians, and which he encouraged all the Corinthians to earnestly desire. I must now give my reasons for thinking so.

Criteria for Accepting a Contribution to a Prayer Meeting as a "Prophecy"

I understand prophecy as a message that is in some real sense a word from the Lord. It is what the Lord wants the group to hear, and not merely what the speaker thinks would be an appropriate message to give. And therefore, if we are going to speak of prophecy, I believe we have to speak of some kind of inspiration as its source. A person should not present his contribution to a prayer meeting as a prophecy unless he is convinced that his message really comes from the Lord and is not just the fruit of his own reflections. Obviously, this subjective conviction needs to be confirmed by the discernment of the group, but at least the speaker ought to feel confident that what he has to say is from the Lord and that he has received it in order to share it with the group. Let us now look at the criteria the group can use in its discernment.

I would distinguish between *negative* and *positive* criteria, and between criteria regarding the *speaker* and those regarding the *message*.

Negative criteria are factors that would rule out, or at least cast grave doubt on, the presence of genuine prophecy. Positive criteria are factors that would favor accepting a word as prophecy. But this does not mean that the presence of positive criteria can always allow one to make a certain judgment that what has been said is really a word from the Lord. Very often, further confirmation of the message should be sought from other reliable signs of God's will. This is extremely important if the prophecy should be directive, that is, if it points toward a specific course of action that the group or certain individuals should follow.

Criteria Regarding the Speaker. In order to apply criteria regarding the speaker, it is, of course, essential that the speaker be a person well known to the group. For this reason, great caution has to be taken with regard to prophecies that are spoken by occasional visitors to a prayer meeting.

As negative factors regarding the speaker, I would mention

any signs of the person's being unbalanced or disturbed; any obvious disorder in the person's way of life; or any indication that the person is an attention-seeker, who might, even innocently, adopt a prophetic style of speech simply as a way of getting attention.

Among positive factors, the most important would be the experience of the group that the previous word-ministry of this person has had consistently good effects on the group. I have expressed my opinion above that one should not present his contribution to a prayer meeting as a prophecy without being convinced that what one has to say is really a word from the Lord. I would see it as a positive factor regarding the person, then, if he or she is the kind of person who you can be sure would not "prophesy" without a strong inner conviction of being inspired to do so. It would also be important to know that the speaker is a prayerful person who shows many other signs of being responsive to God's word in his or her own life.

Criteria Regarding the Message. Prophecy should be discerned primarily by the content of the message, and not by the "prophetic style." It would be a serious mistake for a prayer group simply to accept as prophecy any message that is spoken in the style of the biblical prophets, or that is prefaced or concluded by: "Thus says the Lord."

Similarly, the group should not look on the use of biblical or poetic language as a sure sign of prophecy, or on the use of everyday language, even if it betrays the speaker's linguistic limitations, as a negative criterion. If the theory of word-for-word dictation is rightly discarded with regard to biblical inspiration, it is all the more inappropriate with regard to the inspiration of congregational prophecy.

Among negative criteria regarding the message I would mention its being at variance with scripture or the teaching of the church; its being contrary to charity, unity, or peace; or its having a negative effect on the group, tending to weaken and disrupt it, rather than to build it up in love.

On the other hand, it is not sufficient as a positive criterion of genuine prophecy that the message simply be true, timely, or appropriate. A good homily can be all of these things and still not be prophecy. To be discerned as prophecy, the message must come to the group as a word from the Lord, and not just from the mind of the speaker. A real word from the Lord will have a power and an effectiveness that a merely human word will not have. A word from the Lord not only *says*, it *does*. If it is a word of consolation, it really consoles. If it is a word of rebuke, it really convicts and moves to repentance.

The positive criterion of prophecy, then, is its effectiveness in building up the group to which it is given. Genuine prophecy will awaken a response in the group that merely human exhortations will not have. The surest sign will be the way it contributes to the spiritual growth and maturity of the body. And so we end with the criterion that the Lord himself has given us for judging prophets and prophecies: "You will know them by their fruits" (Mt 7:16).

EIGHT

The Gift of Tongues

THERE ARE THOUSANDS of Christians in the world today who have found that they can speak, pray, and sing in a new, unintelligible "language" which even they themselves do not understand, and who believe that in doing this they are exercising the charismatic gift of tongues of which St. Paul speaks in his First Letter to the Corinthians. This practice and belief are undoubtedly the most distinctive feature of pentecostalism and the charismatic renewal.

It is my experience that questions about the gift of tongues will inevitably come up in any discussion of the charismatic renewal. The first question to which I shall address myself in this chapter is: Is modern tongue-speaking, as practiced in the charismatic renewal, really the same gift of tongues that St. Paul talks about in 1 Corinthians?[1]

Perhaps I should first explain why I do not ask whether modern tongue-speaking is the same phenomenon which Luke tells us accompanied the descent of the Holy Spirit on the Apostles at Pentecost (Acts 2:4-13). The reason for this is that almost all modern exegetes agree that our understanding of the New Testament gift of tongues should be based on what St. Paul tells us about it in 1 Corinthians, rather than on Luke's description of what happened at Pentecost. First of all, Paul is simply a more reliable witness than Luke with regard to this phenomenon. Paul not only witnessed speaking in tongues at Corinth, but also spoke in tongues himself, as he reminded the Corinthians (1 Cor 14:18). On the other hand, Luke was surely not an eyewitness of what happened at Jerusalem on that first

Christian Pentecost. His description of this event is based on tradition.

Most exegetes agree that Luke intends to say that the disciples were speaking the praises of God in a variety of foreign languages, understood by people who had lived in the regions where these languages were spoken. Kremer believes that this "speaking in foreign languages" was already part of the Christian tradition about Pentecost with which Luke worked.[2] It is at least probable that this tradition was influenced by the fact that in some contemporary Jewish circles Pentecost was being celebrated as the feast of the Covenant, and by rabbinic legends about the promulgation of the Sinai Covenant in the seventy languages of the all the nations of the world.[3]

The question as to how literally we should take Luke's description of the tongues of Pentecost as a miraculous speaking of real foreign languages comes down to a question of the literary genre to which this passage belongs. One cannot ignore Haenchen's warning: "We misuse Luke's account of Pentecost when we make believe that it offers us a documentary film of the beginnings of the Christian mission, instead of confining ourselves to the essential theological pronouncements which it embodies."[4] In any case, we are surely on safe ground when we follow the lead of modern exegetes in basing our understanding of the gift of tongues on 1 Corinthians, rather than on Acts 2.

For this reason we are asking what reasons there are for believing that modern tongue-speaking is the same phenomenon as Corinthian glossolalia. What I propose to do is to compare what St. Paul says about speaking in tongues with what modern tongue-speakers are experiencing. I shall begin with the study of what St. Paul tells us about the gift of tongues as it was experienced in the Christian community of Corinth around the middle of the first century.

Corinthian Glossolalia as Described by St. Paul (1 Cor 12-14)

At the outset of this discussion of Corinthian glossolalia, two observations must be made. The first is that Paul is discussing glossolalia with people who are already thoroughly familiar with it. It is not his intention to describe or explain it, as he would if it had been something new or strange to his readers. Any description of this phenomenon is incidental to his purpose, which is rather to moderate the Corinthians' esteem of this gift and to regulate their use of it in their assemblies. Since Paul's remarks are intended for those familiar with glossolalia, it is not surprising that this section, and especially chapter 14, has remained obscure to interpreters, and that it has given rise to quite differing explanations of what it meant to "speak in tongues."

While there are some modern exegetes who maintain that Corinthian glossolalia was the speaking of unlearned foreign languages,[5] by far the more common view today is the one expressed in the translation adopted in the New English Bible, where the word "tongues" is rendered "ecstatic utterance," "tongues of ecstasy," and other similiar expressions. My second observation is that Paul nowhere explicitly tells us either that the "tongues" were real foreign languages, or that tongue-speakers were in a state of ecstasy when they exercised their gift. Both of these views are interpretations that go beyond the explicit witness of Paul's text. For the present, therefore, it is my intention to prescind from both of these judgments about glossolalia, and to concentrate on what Paul actually does tell us about it. Subsequently we may be in a position to judge which (if either) of the two current interpretations is correct. My interpretation of what Paul tells us about glossolalia will be stated in several assertions, the first of which is: *Corinthian glossolalia was articulate speech that at least resembled the speaking of a real language.*

My first reason for this assertion is based on Paul's use of the word *glōssa* (tongue). In current Greek usage, the word *glōssa* had three meanings: 1) the tongue as a physical organ; 2) language; and 3) an obscure, archaic, obsolete, or foreign word or expression needing explanation. The first and third of these meanings are ruled out by the way that Paul uses *glōssa* both in the singular and in the plural. For, if *glōssa* meant the tongue as an organ of speech, it would make no sense to speak, as Paul does, of an individual speaking "with tongues" (e.g. 1 Cor 14:5). On the other hand, if *glōssa* meant an obscure word or expression, it would make sense to use the plural of this noun, but not the singular in the way that Paul does when he speaks of saying ten thousand words "in a *glōssa*" (1 Cor 14:19). So, of the three meanings of *glōssa,* the only one that makes sense when used as Paul uses it in both the singular and the plural is "language"; one may speak both "in a language" and "in languages."

The second reason in support of this view is also found in 1 Corinthians 14:19, where Paul at least envisions the possibility of saying ten thousand *words* "in a tongue." If glossolalia were mere inarticulate muttering, groaning, or the like, Paul would not have described it as "speaking words." Third, the "tongues of men and angels" of 1 Corinthians 13:1 can hardly be other than "languages"; certainly neither of the other two meanings of *glōssa* would be appropriate here.

While these reasons suggest that Corinthian glossolalia was not merely the making of inarticulate sounds, but must have resembled human speech sufficiently to justify calling it "language," it would be premature to conclude that the "tongues" were real foreign languages. We shall return to this question a bit later on.

Our second assertion is: *Corinthian glossolalia was unintelligible not only to the hearers but also to the tongue-speaker himself.* The fact that tongue-speech was unintelligible to the hearers provides the basis of Paul's whole argument in 1 Corinthians 14 showing the inferiority of the gift of tongues to the gift of prophecy, an inferiority that is based precisely on the unintelligibility of what is spoken in tongues, as compared with the intelligibility of what is said in prophecy. That tongue-speech was unintelligible even to the one speaking is clear from 14:13-14: "Therefore, he who speaks in a tongue should pray for the power to interpret. For if I pray in a tongue, my spirit prays but my mind is unfruitful." Paul's exhortation to the tongue-speaker to "pray that he might interpret" shows that the power to interpret was a distinct gift, which might be received by the glossolalist himself, as here, or by someone else in the assembly, as suggested by 14:27-28. However the gift of "interpretation" is to be understood (we shall return to this question later on), there can be no doubt that without this complementary gift, glossolalia by itself remained unintelligible.

Corinthian glossolalia was primarily a way of praying. While, as we have pointd out, Paul does not set out to describe glossolalia as he would have to those unfamiliar with it, a careful reading of what he does say about it suggests that he saw it primarily as a form of prayer. This assertion is based on the following verses of 1 Corinthians 14.

Verse 2 says that the one who speaks in tongues is speaking to God rather than to men. This means more than simply that God is the only one who understands what the tongue-speaker is saying. That "speaking to God" really means prayer is suggested by what Paul says in verse 4: "He who speaks in a tongue edifies himself." There is no reason to take this as ironic or sarcastic; even though Paul clearly prefers that one do something that edifies the community as well as oneself, still it is not a bad thing to build oneself up spiritually by one's own speaking to God.

In verses 14-17 Paul mentions various ways in which glossolalia was used: in *praying* (vv. 14-15); in *singing*—in the context this would undoubtedly be prayerful singing, as of psalms or hymns (v. 15); in *blessing* (v. 16) and in *giving thanks* (vv. 16-17). The fact that the word for "thanksgiving" here is *eucharistia* has sometimes been taken to mean that at Corinth the eucharistic prayer itself might have been spoken in glossolalia, but this is very doubtful. However, there can be no doubt that "blessing" and "giving thanks" are forms of prayer, to which the listener would be expected to give his "amen."

In verse 28 we are again told that the tongue-speaker, if he cannot speak to men, can use his "tongue" in speaking to God; in fact, Paul urges him to do so. This is surely to be understood as an exhortation to prayer, and indeed, as we shall now point out, to private prayer in tongues.

In Paul's view, glossolalia was primarily useful in private prayer. As we have already seen, one who "speaks to God" in tongues "edifies himself" (vv. 2, 4). On the other hand, public prayer in tongues, without the corresponding gift of interpretation, was to be discouraged, because the listener, not knowing the meaning of what was said, could not say "amen" (v. 16) and would not be edified by it (v. 17). In the absence of a person with the gift of interpretation, Paul directs the tongue-speaker to "be silent in the assembly and to speak to himself and to God" (v. 28). To a modern reader this might suggest that the glossolalist, while refraining from speaking out in the assembly, is to pray silently in tongues while the meeting is going on around him. But it is much more likely that Paul is drawing a line between what the tongue-speaker does "in the assembly" and what he does "by himself"; in the assembly he is to be silent, but when by himself he is to *speak* (the Greek word here surely means audible utterance), and the one to whom he will speak is God. A number of modern commentators have recognized that Paul is here distinguishing between the public and private use of prayer in tongues, rather than between audible and silent prayer during the assembly.[6]

Furthermore, the very severe restrictions which Paul placed upon the use of glossolalia in the assembly (vv. 27-28: it is to be used only when there is someone to interpret, and even then by no more than three speakers) suggest that Paul saw this gift as useful primarily in private prayer. For, on the other hand, he expressed the wish that all have this gift (v. 5); in the light of the restrictions which he himself had placed on its use in public, one can only conclude that he wanted them to have it for use in private prayer. Finally, we have Paul's testimony about his own use of this gift (vv. 18-19): "I thank God that I speak in tongues more than you all; nevertheless, in church [i.e. in the assembly] I would rather speak five words with my mind, than ten thousand words in a tongue." If we take Paul literally, he is saying not merely that he has the gift of tongues, but that he actually speaks in tongues more than the Corinthians do, and he thanks God that he does so. But he has also determined not to use this gift in the assembly. When, we may ask, did he do all the tongue-speaking he thanks God for, if not in his private prayer?

We can sum up what we have so far learned about Corinthian glossolalia by saying that St. Paul describes it as language-like human speech, unintelligible both to speaker and to hearers, useful primarily as a form of private prayer. We must now examine the grounds on which commentators have based the two interpretations that are current today: that of speaking unlearned foreign languages, and that of ecstatic utterance. First we shall ask: *did St. Paul understand glossolalia to be the speaking of unlearned foreign languages?*

The affirmative answer to this question has been argued most emphatically and extensively by R.H. Gundry.[7] Let us look at the arguments which Gundry has offered for his position. His first argument is based on the use of the word *glōssa*. Gundry insists (rightly, we believe) that of the three possible meanings of this word, the one that corresponds to the way the word is used in these chapters of 1 Corinthians is "language." As I have already said, I believe that the use of this word is a good argument in favor of the view that glossolalia was articulate human speech, at least resembling the speaking of an unknown language. The word *glōssa* describes the phenomenon; it tells us what glossolalia sounded like. But it seems to me that more solid evidence is needed before we can draw the conclusion that the glossolalists were speaking real foreign languages, or that this is what St. Paul thought they were doing.

Gundry's second argument is based on the use of the word *diermêneuô* and its cognates to describe what the person with the gift of "interpretation of tongues" did. Following Davies, Gundry argues that in the Septuagint and in the New Testament, this word most frequently means "translate." If, then, the tongues could be translated, they must have been real foreign languages. But here again, the conclusion seems to go beyond the evidence. When one person spoke out in what sounded like a strange language, and another person followed this with a prayer or message in plain Greek, it would be only natural to say that the second person "interpreted" what the first had said. But this would be true whether the "interpreter" actually understood the language that had been spoken, or whether he were given a prophetic insight into the sense of the prayer or message without actually understanding the "tongue" as such. If the "tongue" sounded like a language, then the "interpretation" would also have sounded like a translation, and that, it seems to me, is all that the use of these words necessarily implies.

Finally, Gundry argues, Paul's use of the analogy between a tongue-speaker and a foreigner speaking his own language "should clear away any vestige of doubt that he thinks of the gift of tongues as miraculous speaking in unlearned human languages."[8] But, as a look at the context will show, Paul makes use of two analogies in this passage (14:7-11), not only with the foreigner speaking his own language, but also with a musical instrument that makes an indistinct sound. Neither analogy should be pressed beyond the precise point that Paul wishes to make: namely, the unintelligibility of glossolalia, and hence its uselessness to those who hear it.

Having considered the arguments which Gundry has advanced in favor of his view we must look at the reasons which have convinced most modern commentators that Corinthian glossolalia was not the speaking of unlearned foreign languages. The first reason is that the burden of proof lies on those who maintain that it did involve such a prodigy, and the arguments which have been advanced for this view are not convincing. Second, there is Paul's insistence on the unintelligibility of tongues. Paul does not seem to envision even the possibility that someone might happen to be present who could naturally understand the language being spoken, a possibility that would not seem utterly remote in a trading center like Corinth.[9] In any case, there is not the slightest hint, in anything Paul says, in favor of the view that the value of this gift lay in its convincing power as a miracle of being able to communicate in a language one had never learned. Rather, as Paul states, "One who speaks in a tongue speaks not to men but to God" (14:2).

If, then, there are no sufficient reasons for holding that

Corinthian glossolalia was the speaking of unlearned foreign languages, we must now ask how solid the grounds are for the other opinion, which enjoys the favor of the majority of modern exegetes. *Was Corinthian glossolalia "ecstatic utterance"?*

A preliminary question to be asked is: what is meant by "ecstasy"? G.B. Cutten has offered the following description, with which I believe most would agree: "In ecstasy there is a condition of emotional exaltation, in which the one who experiences it is more or less oblivious of the external world, and loses to some extent his self-consciousness and his power of rational thought and self-control."[10] E.B. Allo, who believes that tongue-speakers were *"saisis par l'extase,"* is convinced that in their state of ecstasy they were no longer in control of what they did or said.[11] He bases his judgment as to the ecstatic nature of Corinthian glossolalia on what Paul says about the inactivity of the mind in this kind of prayer: "For if I pray in a tongue, my spirit prays but my mind is unfruitful"; when a person prays "in a tongue," he is praying "with the spirit," but not "with the mind" (14:14-15, 19).[12]

Here is the question we must ask: is ecstasy the only reasonable explanation of what Paul says about the respective roles of "spirit" and "mind" in glossolalia? One thing is abundantly clear: even the glossolalist himself did not understand the meaning of what he was saying. At least in this sense he was not praying "with his mind." From this premise the conclusion is certainly warranted that glossolalia was not normal human speech; it was clearly not the verbalization of mental concepts.

But what does Paul mean by saying that "when I pray in a tongue, it is my spirit that prays," that the glossolalist prays and sings "with the spirit," or that he "utters mysteries with the spirit"? In Paul's view, is what is done "with the spirit" necessarily done in ecstasy? Allo's own explanation of what Paul means by "spirit" would not seem to bear out such a conclusion. If the "spirit" with which the glossolalist prays is, as Allo describes it, "the highest part of the human intelligence, operating under the transitory influence of the Holy Spirit,"[13] I fail to see why the fact that such operations of the "spirit" exclude the discursive operations of the mind leads necessarily to the conclusion that they involve a state of ecstasy. Would such an argument not also lead to the conclusion that all non-discursive, non-conceptual prayer is necessarily ecstatic?

In any case, there remains a serious difficulty against the theory that Corinthian glossolalists exercised their gift in a state of ecstasy. As we have noted, Allo understands ecstasy as a state in which a person is no longer in control of what he does or says. But in 1 Corinthians 14:27-28 Paul gave explicit regulations for the exercise of glossolalia in the assembly: "If any speak in a tongue, let there be only two or at most three, and each in turn, and let one interpret. But if there is no one to interpret, let each of them keep silence in the assembly and speak to himself and to God." Paul clearly takes it for granted that those who speak in tongues can and should control the exercise of their gift. Furthermore, we have Paul's own testimony to his control over his own gift of tongues. He had this gift in abundance, but he chose not to exercise it in the assembly (v. 19). Here at least was one genuine glossolalist who could follow the rules he himself laid down for the use of this gift. Paul's use of the future tense at 14:15 is another indication that he expected the glossolalist to be free to choose, in any particular circumstance, whether he would "pray with his spirit" or "pray with his mind."

An argument that has been offered to prove that glossolalia must have been an ecstatic phenomenon is the warning which Paul gives in verse 23: "If, therefore, the whole church assembles and all speak in tongues, and outsiders or unbelievers enter, will they not say that you are mad?" However, it is clear that Paul is setting up an unreal hypothesis, namely, that all are speaking in tongues, with no one saying anything intelligible, and no one interpreting the tongues. Surely such a disorderly spectacle would justify the impression that the whole crowd had gone mad. But Paul himself had previously made it clear that in any given community not all had the gift of tongues (12:30: "Do all speak with tongues?"). The question, therefore, is whether, from the impression that would very likely be created by a disordered exercise of glossolalia, one can rightly conclude to the nature of glossolalia itself. In other words, would the individual glossolalists speaking, as Paul directs, one at a time, and only when there is someone to interpret, also have created the impression of madness—or of being carried away in ecstasy? In this case, could Paul have concluded his exhortation on the use of the gifts with the direction: "Do not forbid speaking in tongues, but all things should be done decently and in order" (14:39-40)?

Having, up to this point, analyzed Paul's description of Corinthian glossolalia, we sum up our conclusions: that it was not the production merely of inarticulate sighs or groans, but rather of language-like speech, unintelligible both to the speaker and the hearers; that it was seen by Paul as a form of prayer, primarily useful in private; that it was not the speaking of real foreign languages; and that it was not the product of ecstasy, if we understand ecstasy as a condition in which a person loses rational control over his actions. It is now time to ask whether modern tongue-speaking, such as is practiced in the charismatic renewal, is substantially the same kind of thing that St. Paul was talking about.

Tongue-Speaking in the Charismatic Renewal

The distinctive belief of the Pentecostal churches is that every Christian who has been "baptized in the Spirit" will have spoken in tongues at least on that occasion, and it is expected that for many this will be an abiding gift, to be used both in private prayer and in community worship.

While Catholics involved in the charismatic renewal do not, as a rule, subscribe to the belief that every "baptism in the Spirit" must be authenticated by glossolalia, many of them do encourage those seeking the "baptism" to pray for the gift of tongues, as the "normal and expected sign" that the Holy Spirit is now working in their lives in a new and more powerful way.[14] One significant fact revealed by the questionnaire which Joseph Fichter administered to American Catholic lay-people involved in the charismatic renewal is that eighty-six percent of his respondents reported that they had received the gift of tongues.[15] It should be noted, however, that Fichter admits that his respondents did not represent a random sample of participants in the renewal, but rather a selection of the more fully committed members of Catholic prayer groups.[16] But even with this proviso, it seems safe to conclude that a very high percentage of the active and dedicated members of "charismatic" prayer groups will pray in tongues.

Scientific Descriptions of Tongue-Speech

Given the large numbers of Pentecostals and neo-pentecostals who speak in tongues, there is now no lack of evidence on which linguistic scientists can base their description and analysis of this phenomenon. I shall report briefly on the studies made by Willian J. Samarin and Virginia H. Hine,[17] both of which are based on extensive firsthand observation by people trained to observe and analyze human behavior.

Empirical studies of glossolalia begin with the premise that glossolalia is that kind of vocal utterance which people in the Pentecostal churches and the charismatic renewal practice and accept as "speaking in tongues." This kind of speech, which he can observe, record, and analyze, is the known quantity for the empirical scientist; it is on this alone that he bases his description of glossolalia. William J. Samarin, in his book *Tongues of Men and Angels, The Religious Language of Pentecostalism,* has offered several definitions of glossolalia, all of which seem to come down to saying that glossolalia is human speech that sounds like real language, but when analyzed is found not to be real language.[18] Because it sounds so much like a real language, it is not surprising that the majority of glossolalists interviewed by Samarin believed their tongue-speech to be a real language, even though they did not know what language it was or understand it.[19] Virginia Hine reported that glossolalic utterances "are usually patterned sufficiently so that the tongue speech of one individual may be distinguished from that of another. Often one tongue-speaker uses two or more different patternings or 'languages.' "[20] Given the often remarkably language-like sound of glossolalia, a person without training in linguistics might have difficulty in deciding whether a tape-recording was of glossolalia or of a real language, one, of course, with which the listener was unfamiliar.

Why, then, do linguists such as Samarin insist that no sample of glossolalia which they have ever analyzed has proved to be real language? How can they exclude the possibility that it might be some ancient or exotic language unknown even to them? The answer, as Samarin explains, is that every language, in order to be language at all, has to be a system of vocal symbols internally organized in a patterned way and related arbitrarily to the external world. "Language is so systematic, in fact, that man is hardly ingenious enough to disguise it to the extent that another human being cannot decode it."[21] If the sounds made by a tongue-speaker were real words, and if what sound like sentences were really the arrangement of such words into meaningful sequences, then the resulting language would inevitably have a consistent pattern and structure that would enable a trained linguist to identify this as a "code," and eventually to decode it. Without going into the technical details, we can simply accept the judgment of the expert in his own field: "When the full apparatus of linguistic science comes to bear on glossolalia, this turns out to be only a facade of language—although at times a very good one indeed. For when we comprehend what language is, we must conclude that no glossa, no matter how well constructed, is a specimen of human language, because it is neither internally organized nor systematically related to the world man perceives."[22]

To deny that the "tongues" are real languages in the proper sense of the term, however, is not to deny that glossolalic utterances can be, and often are, expressive of feeling and thought. If one takes "language" in the broad sense as "any means, vocal or other, of expressing feeling or thought," then one can speak of the "language" of music, of painting, or the dance. In an analogous sense one can also speak of glossolalia as a "language of prayer and praise," because it can be expressive of, and communicate to others, the glossolalist's internal attitude of prayer. But, as Samarin points out, "in glossolalia it is the total speech event, not its parts, that is primarily correlated to the 'world,' or, more accurately, with a person's emotional response to experience."[23]

James R. Jaquith has described glossolalia as a form of "non-linguistic communicative behavior," and in this respect has judged it to be analogous, in its manner of communication, to religious ritual that is celebrated in a "sacred" language unknown to the congregation, and to opera being sung in a language unknown to the audience.[24] In these cases, meaning is being expressed and communicated, not via the semantic "code" of Latin or Italian, but through the total religious or musical event. At the same time, of course, Jaquith agrees with Samarin and other linguists who have analyzed glossolalia, that "we are dealing here not with language, but with verbalizations which superficially resemble language in certain of its structural aspects."[25]

In view of this agreement of competent linguists that "tongues" are not real languages, what is to be thought of the many accounts published in the literature of the pentecostal movement of instances in which a glossolalic utterance has been recognized as spoken in a foreign language unknown to the speaker but known to someone who happened to be present? Technically this is known as xenoglossia. To my knowledge, no case of genuine xenoglossia has been verified to the satisfaction of scientific observers. I agree with them that a healthy skepticism is justified until there is adequate evidence that real xenoglossia has taken place. One has to keep in mind that there are many factors that could lead people sincerely to believe that they had witnessed a case of xenoglossia when what had actually occurred would not satisfy the scientists' definition of it.

On the other hand, I do not exclude the possibility that some of the episodes that are described in pentecostal literature may actually involve cases of genuine xenoglossia. Since I believe that God does intervene in human affairs in ways that are sometimes quite extraordinary, I am prepared to believe that he might use someone's tongue-speech as the means of bringing a person to conversion, by having him hear a call to repentance or faith spoken to him in his own language, by a speaker who did not know that language and was not even aware that he was speaking it. I do not reject the idea that God might choose to use the gift of tongues in that way in a particular case. On the other hand, none of the episodes that I have read about suggests that the tongue-speaker's glossolalia was habitually the real language that it was recognized to be on the occasion when the xenoglossia took place. And, in any case, I do not think that such occurrences, even if they could be adequately documented, would justify the belief that glossolalic tongues are ordinarily real languages, in the face of the evidence adduced by linguists to the contrary.

At this point it should be noted that the recognition of a real language being spoken by a tongue-speaker is not what is meant by the "interpretation of tongues." In the charismatic renewal it is understood as normal that neither the tongue-speaker nor the one who gives the "interpretation" actually understands the "language" in which the message in tongues is spoken. The "interpretation" is not claimed to be a translation, in the ordinary sense of the word.[26] I shall return to the question of the "interpretation of tongues" at the end of this chapter.

A Gift for Prayer

We have seen that for St. Paul the gift of tongues was primarily a gift to be used in prayer, and that while it had a limited place in community worship, it was mainly to be used in private prayer. Undoubtedly Paul's prescriptions for the use of tongues have had considerable influence on people in the charismatic renewal, who take their Bible very seriously and even sometimes too literally. On the other hand, I do not believe that the mere intention to follow the rule laid down in scripture could account for the fact that, for so many people, "speaking in tongues" has been the key that seems to have unlocked the door to personal contact with God in prayer. It would be easy to multiply testimonies to the value of tongues for personal prayer, from the writings of representatives of the renewal. The following statement of L. Christenson is typical:

> One speaks in tongues, for the most part, in his private devotions. *This is by far its most important use and value.* It offers the believer a glorious new dimension in prayer. . . . Although one does not know what he is saying as he speaks in tongues, he does have a clear sense that he is praying to God. The heightened awareness of God's presence is one of the greatest blessings one receives through this experience.[27]

Another Protestant pastor, J.R. Williams, writes in the same vein:

> Tongues are primarily for devotional use. Since they basically edify (build up) the believer in his faith, most persons pray in tongues privately (or with a few others) and find great joy and strength in so doing. Praying with the Spirit becomes the fruitful base for praying with the mind, and it is in the alternation and interplay of these two dimensions of prayer and praise that spiritual growth and maturation takes place.[28]

For Arnold Bittlinger, the primary value of tongues lies in its being a vehicle for the "outpouring of the heart to God," for "prayer from the heart" and not just from the mind.[29] W. Hollenweger sees the important role of tongues to be that it offers "an opportunity for prayer in a non-rational meditative language. This is a significant prayer experience on the one hand for people unaccustomed to abstract discourse and on the other hand for academic people who are intellectually top-heavy."[30] George Montague, a Catholic biblical scholar who speaks of the value of praying in tongues from the background not only of scripture but also from his own personal experience, has written:

The gift is primarily non-rational prayer ("The one who speaks in a tongue speaks not to men but to God" [1 Cor 14:2]). Artless, it uses no phrenetic energy in formulation. . . . Not that I am suddenly given a miraculous lingual mechanism—the mechanism is as simple as singing in the shower or humming a line of nonsense. But the gift is to let go inwardly and outwardly sufficiently to allow this foolishness of babbling praise to well forth. And this becomes the gift of one's personal prayer-language before God."[31]

Is Modern Glossolalia "Ecstatic Utterance"?

So far we have seen that modern glossolalia resembles the New Testament "gift of tongues" in its being language-like human speech but not real language, unintelligible both to the speaker himself and to his hearers, that is found to be primarily useful as a way of praying to God, particularly in private prayer. We must now ask what answer both tongue-speakers themselves and scientific observers of this phenomenon give to the question whether this kind of speech is the product of some such altered mental state as ecstasy or trance.

A good summary of the present state of the discussion among scientific observers of glossolalia is given by O'Connell and Bryant:

There are all sorts of theoretical and inferred impedimenta added to the phenomenon by various writers, mostly by means of a disturbingly inadequate use of scientific data and reasoning. One such inference is that glossolalia is necessarily an altered state of consciousness, hyperarousal dissociation, trance, a behavior the speaker himself does not hear and from which he has no feedback. The most recent proponent of this position is Goodman.[32] Samarin's comment is simply that "in fact an altered state of consciousness rarely accompanies the production of glossolalia among Christians."[33] Hine is in agreement with Samarin on this point.[34]

Virginia Hine was a member of a research team which carried out an anthropological study of the pentecostal movement under the direction of Dr. Luther Gerlach of the University of Minnesota. She reports the findings of this research on the question of the mental state of glossolalists as follows:

> Glossolalia in the Pentecostal context is sometimes associated with an altered mental state, with some degree of dissociation or trance. It occasionally involves involuntary motor activity, or, rarely, complete loss of consciousness. These behaviors are most common during the initial experience of glossolalia which usually is associated with the Baptism of the Holy Spirit, a subjective experience of being filled with or possessed by the Holy Spirit. Subsequent use of the "gift of tongues" is most often independent of any altered mental state or trance behavior.[35]

William Samarin has expressed his views on this question in the following passage of his book *Tongues of Men and Angels*:

> We have come to the same conclusions independently, but we would agree that the acquisition of charismatic or Pentecostal glossolalia is *sometimes* associated with *some* degree of altered state of consciousness, that this *occasionally* involves motor activity that is involuntary or, *rarely*, a complete loss of consciousness, and that in any case subsequent use of glossolalia (that is, after the initial experience) is *most often indepentent* of dissociative phenomena.[36]

At this point it would be easy, but it hardly seems necessary, to multiply testimonies from people who both speak in tongues themselves and have witnessed many other people do so, to the effect that the use of this gift is not ordinarily accompanied by ecstasy or trance. On the contrary, they know that it is something over which they have conscious control, in the sense that, once having received this gift, they can choose to use it or not in any given circumstance. They can begin and stop at will;

they determine whether to speak audibly or silently, whether to speak or to sing, and so forth. To quote but one author, L. Christenson: "The idea that a speaker in tongues goes off into a kind of religious ecstasy, where he loses emotional and personal control, is contrary both to Scripture and actual experience. The person who exercises this gift is perfectly able to remain in full control of himself and his emotions."[37]

Our study of the evidence, both in the writings of St. Paul and in current experience, has shown that glossolalia, both Corinthian and modern, is unintelligible language-like speech, which is neither the speaking of unlearned foreign languages nor a product of religious ecstasy, but is found by its users to be helpful as a way of praying, especially in private. The conclusion seems justified that we are witnessing nowadays a religious phenomenon that is substantially the same as that of which St. Paul speaks in 1 Corinthians 12-14. On the basis of this conclusion, we are now in a better position to understand why St. Paul thanked God that he had this gift, and why he expressed the wish that all might have it (1 Cor 14:5, 18). For today thousands of Christians can bear witness to the fruits which this way of praying has borne in their lives. Many questions still remain as to why this way of praying is so beneficial. But the obscurity of the "how" and "why" cannot negate the reality of the fact that for a great many this has been the key that unlocked the door to a new experience of God in prayer.

In the following section I shall offer my own understanding of what people are doing when they "speak in tongues," how they come to do this, and why speaking in tongues proves for many of them to be a new gift of prayer.

What Are People Doing When They "Speak in Tongues"?

Perhaps it would be helpful first to say what they are *not* doing: they are not consciously and deliberately making up nonsense syllables and stringing them together so as to produce a pseudo-language. This is what a person might do if he had attended a meeting in which he heard people speaking in tongues, and afterwards attempted to imitate what it sounded like. Such deliberate production of a nonsense language differs from genuine glossolalia in an essential point: in genuine glossolalia the person speaking does not consciously choose the sounds he is going to make. It is true that he deliberately chooses whether to speak in tongues or not, and he has to use his vocal organs in order to produce this kind of speech, just as he would in ordinary speech; but he leaves the choice of what sounds he is going to make to what I believe is a subconscious level of self. (Others believe that it is the Holy Spirit who "supplies a new language,'" but I see no sufficient reason to have recourse to so supernaturalist an explanation.) Whereas the deliberate production of a pseudo-language, at least for many people, might involve considerable effort, it is typical of genuine glossolalia that it flows out without any effort, and can be continued for long periods of time without fatigue.

It might seem contradictory to say that in genuine glossolalia the person chooses to speak but does not choose what sounds he is going to make. Perhaps an analogy would help to clarify this. Suppose a person becomes aware that he has been daydreaming. At this point it would be possible for him to choose to continue to daydream, and then his daydreaming would become voluntary. But this would not necessarily mean that he would begin consciously to choose the images that would pass before his "mind's eye." He could simply allow his imagination to continue to wander as it was before. In other words, a person may consciously choose to daydream, and at the same time allow the choice of phantasms to be made at a sub-conscious level of self.

If I am not mistaken, the production of genuine glossolalia involves something analogous to this. In fact, I would push the analogy one step further and say that as everyone has a natural capacity to daydream, it is my belief that everyone also has a natural capacity to produce genuine glossolalia. In my opinion, the gift of tongues does not consist in a new capacity to speak in a way that others, lacking such a gift, could not speak. I am convinced that to begin to speak in tongues means simply to activate a latent capacity which probably everyone has. The next question is: how is this latent capacity activated?

How Do People Come to Speak in Tongues?

We have seen evidence above that a high percentage of fully committed participants in the Catholic charismatic renewal, at least as this has developed in the United States, will speak in tongues, and that there is also a very high correlation between tongue-speaking and having been "baptized in the Spirit." We are asking now why it is that the activation of the latent capacity to produce glossolalia is so often associated with the experience of being "baptized in the Spirit." In my opinion, one has to reckon with many human and natural factors, as well as with the operation of divine grace, in explaining this association.

It seems to me that one of the human factors here is the relative stress that is laid on the gift of tongues in the preparation of newcomers for the prayer for "baptism in the Spirit." Probably the most commonly used method for such preparation, at least in the Catholic charismatic renewal in English-speaking countries, is called the "Life in the Spirit Seminars." One has only to read the *Team Manual for the Life in the Spirit Seminars* to see how much stress is laid on the importance of the candidate's speaking in tongues when he or she is "baptized in the Spirit."[38]

For many people, the first experience of speaking in tongues requires the overcoming of a natural resistance to "letting go" of personal control over what sounds are going to come out when one speaks. Especially for people who tend to maintain a very tight control over themselves, there can be a deep-seated repugnance to such a surrender of control over one's own speech. There is a kind of "stepping out into the dark" in beginning to speak without knowing what kind of sounds one is going to make, or knowing how foolish it might sound. For all these reasons, before one actually "takes the plunge" and begins to speak in tongues, one has to have a strong desire to do this.

Clearly, one of the purposes of the "Life in the Spirit Seminars," as presented in the *Team Manual,* is to create such a desire. The motive which the *Manual* presents is that speaking in tongues will give the person "a clear experience of what it means to have the Holy Spirit work through him" (p. 147). In other words, speaking in tongues is presented as an important proof of the Spirit's new presence and working in the person. The approach is: "If you really want this new presence of the Holy Spirit strongly enough, then you should also want this experiential sign of his working within you."

If the person comes to desire and expect that he will receive this sign when he is prayed with for his "baptism in the Spirit," then given the encouragement and coaching which the "team members" are advised to give, it is not surprising that a high percentage of the people who go through the "Life in the Spirit Seminars" begin to speak in tongues either when they are prayed for, or within a short time after they are "baptized in the Spirit."

Another factor that must be taken into consideration is the role which speaking in tongues plays in many prayer groups, as the tangible sign of full commitment to the charismatic renewal. In groups where glossolalia has such a role, no matter how faithfully a person may attend the meetings, there will seem to be something lacking in his commitment to the renewal, and his wholehearted participation in it, until he has taken the "bridge-burning" step of speaking in tongues. This is the "commitment act" which sociologists recognize as characteristic of the whole pentecostal movement.[39]

It is likely, then, that the question whether a person will begin to speak in tongues when he is prayed with for his "baptism in the Spirit" will also depend on how important a sign of commitment speaking in tongues is considered to be in this particular group, and how deeply the person really wants to be committed to the charismatic renewal, as this groups represents it.

It is true that the factors I have thus far considered could all be described as human and natural ones. However, I am convinced that in many cases there is a genuine work of divine grace involved in a person's beginning to speak in tongues. The act of "letting go," of "yielding" to tongues, can be truly symbolic of a much deeper surrender to the Lord. It can be the "breakthrough" that was needed in order for the person to give his life fully to God. The willingness to make a fool of oneself can be expressive of a readiness for conversion, for the transformation that a new outpouring of the Holy Spirit will produce in one's life.

I see a work of grace in the desire for such a transforming gift of the Spirit, and in the attitude of openness to the consequences which such a transformation could have in one's life. The readiness to take the "bridge-burning" step of speaking in tongues can be truly expressive of this readiness for conversion. In this case, it seems to me that there can be real grace involved in "taking the plunge" into speaking in tongues—not in itself, so much, as in what this signifies, when it really does express such an attitude of surrender to the work of God in one's life.

The proof, of course, of whether a real "baptism in the Holy Spirit" has taken place will be the subsequent transformation of the person's life, not his speaking in tongues when prayed over. The merely natural factors, I believe, can account adequately for a person's speaking in tongues, but they cannot account for a deep spiritual renewal. Speaking in tongues, then, is a work of grace when it is a sign of such genuine renewal in the Spirit. The phenomenon of speaking in tongues, as such, is not an authenticating sign of spiritual renewal, but itself needs to be authenticated by subsequent evidence that a real spiritual renewal has taken place.

Speaking in Tongues as a Charismatic Gift

I believe that when speaking in tongues is a genuine gift of grace, a "charism," it will prove to be a new gift of prayer, especially for prayer of praise. The question whether speaking in tongues in any particular case is a genuine charism or not can be answered by asking what it does for a person's life of prayer.

The value of this gift of prayer seems to lie in its freeing the depths of the human spirit to express audibly and vocally (that is, with the body as an integral part of the self) what it cannot find words to express in conceptual language. Most people who pray in this way find in their "new tongue" a language of praise, whereby they feel that they can express what otherwise they find inexpressible about God and their desire to praise him for what he is in himself. While for many the effort to put the praise of God into their own words is so difficult that it curbs the flight of the spirit, prayer in tongues offers an effortless way to vocalize their attitude of praise. Prayer in tongues has been called "pre-rational" or "pre-conceptual" prayer, prayer "of the heart" rather than of the mind. I suspect that a closer and more sympathetic study of the current experience of prayer in tongues, by scholars in the field of Christian spirituality, will disclose illuminating analogies between this and other forms of prayer in which "the spirit prays while the mind is at rest."

As one such analogy, I would suggest the relationship between the gift of tongues and the "gift of tears." In both cases, I believe, it is a question of the activation of a natural capacity. Obviously, everyone has the natural capacity for tears; in my opinion everyone also has a latent capacity for glossolalia. The "gift" does not consist in either case in the imparting of a new physical capacity. Further, just as not every kind of weeping qualifies as the "gift of tears," so also, in my opinion, not every kind of glossolalia qualifies as the charismatic gift of tongues.

When does weeping qualify as the "gift of tears"? It seems to me that it is when it both *signifies* and *intensifies* such an attitude as contrition for sins, compassion with the sufferings of Christ, or joy in the experience of consolation. In some mysterious way (bound up, no doubt, with our composite body-soul nature) the fact that my body is sharing in and expressing my inner state of soul means that I—as the whole person—am somehow more contrite than I would be if I were not weeping for my sins.

There is a kind of sacramental efficacy about this sign of tears; it not only signifies, but it sustains and intensifies the contrition, or compassion, or joy which it expresses bodily.

I believe that something analogous to this can be said about tongues. Speaking in tongues is a real gift of grace, a charism, when it has a similar quasi-sacramental kind of efficacy, both to signify and to intensify one's attitude of prayer, especially prayer of praise. One cannot find the appropriate words to "magnify the Lord" with, but one is not thereby prevented from expressing vocally one's inner attitude of praise. One can simply let this effortless "language of praise" flow forth unhindered, knowing that this is genuine praise of God, just as surely as one can know that one's tears are a genuine prayer of contrition.

Perhaps in our over-cerebral approach to prayer we have neglected the important role our bodies can play in expressing and intensifying our prayer. The psalmist exhorts us to "make a joyful noise to the Lord" (Ps 98:4). Just as there are times when there is no better way to pray than just to weep, so also many people have discovered that at times there is no better way to pray than just to "make a joyful noise to the Lord," out of a heart full of thanksgiving and praise.

"Singing in Tongues" and "Jubilation"

The reference to the psalmist's exhortation to "make a joyful noise to the Lord" (a phrase which the Vulgate Latin Bible translates as "jubilate Domino") suggests another analogy that could profitably be pursued, namely, that between what in the charismatic renewal is often called "singing in tongues," and what is known in Christian tradition as "jubilation."

It might be helpful to recall here what I said earlier, when describing some distinctive features of neo-pentecostal groups, namely, that during their meetings there may be moments when their simultaneous vocal prayer will turn into spontaneous singing, with each person forming his or her own melody, either using real words or in tongues, and that in such singing many groups produce a strangely beautiful harmony.

I think it important to note that participation in this kind of singing does not demand that one be producing genuine glossolalia, which by definition is "language-like." In any given group, some will probably be actually singing in tongues, but others can simply begin singing a word like "alleluia" and improvise a melody, ringing the changes on the vowel sounds as they continue to sing. The harmony that often results is an indication of the degree to which the members of the group have learned to listen to one another, and to be sensitive to what is going on in the meeting. Without doubt much will depend on their natural instinct for harmonious sound, but, in my opinion, there are often deeper factors at work that manifest themselves in the quality of the harmony that is produced. The essential factor is the inner attitude which all wish to express in this "singing to the Lord." Usually this will be an attitude of praise and thanksgiving, but at other times it can be an attitude of repentance, or of petition, depending on the circumstances. The union of hearts in the same prayer, whatever it may be, will express itself in the harmony that develops in this kind of spontaneous group singing.

Perhaps there were some who looked on this as just another practice that the charismatic renewal had picked up from the Pentecostals, and that was alien to Catholic tradition. It not seldom happens that people who make judgments about what is traditional are identifying tradition with what they are accustomed to.

In any case, there is thoroughly reliable evidence that a kind of spontaneous congregational singing that is analogous if not identical to modern "singing in the Spirit" was practiced in Christian churches in the patristic age and for many centuries thereafter. The traditional name for this kind of singing was "jubilation." There is a scholarly article on jubilation in the *Dictionnaire de Spiritualité.*[40] E. Ensley has given a popular presentation of much of the same material in his recent book *Sounds of Wonder.*[41]

The name "jubilation" comes from the Latin *jubilatio* (from the verb *jubilare*) which the ancient Latin translations of the

Bible used for the words *alalagmos* and *alalazo* of the Greek Septuagint version, in turn corresponding to the Hebrew *ru'a* and *terou'a*. It was the use of these words in the Psalms which most influenced the Christian practice of "jubilation."[42] This is particularly evident in St. Augustine's commentaries on the Psalms. Each time that these words occurred in a psalm, St. Augustine not only explained what was meant by "jubilation," but he exhorted his congregation to "sing in jubilation." One of the many passages where he does this is in his commentary on Psalm 32, where his version of verse 3 reads: "Cantate in jubilatione" ("Sing in jubilation"). St. Augustine's commentary is as follows:

> What does it mean to sing in jubilation? It means to realize that you cannot express in words what your heart is singing. People who are singing, for example, during the harvest or the vintage or some other such ardent work, who have begun to exult with joy in the words of a song, as if filled with such great joy that they can no longer express it in words, leave off the syllables of words and go into the sound of jubilation. For jubilation is a sound which signifies that the heart is giving utterance to what it cannot say in words. And for whom is such jubilation fitting if not for the ineffable God? For he is ineffable whom one cannot express in words; and if you cannot express Him in words, and yet you cannot remain silent either, then what is left but to sing in jubilation, so that your heart may rejoice without words, and your unbounded joy may not be confined by the limits of syllables."[43]

This practice of improvised, wordless singing is attested by a great many Fathers of the Church, both Greek and Latin, and it did not cease at the close of the patristic age. Up until the ninth century, it was a regular part of the Easter liturgy for the congregation to prolong the last syllable of the Easter *alleluia* with improvised melodies. This was called the *jubilus*, which after the ninth century was replaced by the "sequence," with fixed words and melody.

While the practice of congregational singing in jubilation is not so well attested in later periods of church history, there is a consistent tradition in writings of Christian spirituality, from the medieval to the modern period, which attests to the private practice of wordless, improvised singing as an expression of a spiritual joy that cannot be expressed in words. Both St. Teresa of Avila and St. John of the Cross knew this experience, which they called *júbilo*.[44]

At this point the question may be asked: if there are such obvious similarities between the traditional practice of jubilation, and modern "singing in tongues," how can one explain the fact that the Fathers and other Christian writers who speak of jubilation never seem to have identified it with the New Testament "gift of tongues," or the "singing with the spirit" of which St. Paul speaks in 1 Corinthians 14:15?

If I am not mistaken, the answer to this question lies in the fact that the Fathers, and practically everyone who wrote on this until quite recently, understood the gift of tongues to be the miraculous ability to preach the gospel in foreign languages that one had never learned. Given their mistaken notion of what the gift of tongues really was, it is understandable that they would not identify the wordless singing of jubilation with the New Testament charism. But in our day, when biblical and historical studies on the one hand, and experience on the other, have shed new light on the gift of tongues, we can now see the close analogy between what St. Paul called "singing with the spirit" and what Christian tradition has called "jubilation."

The Interpretation of Tongues

I shall close this chapter with some brief remarks about what is called "the interpretation of tongues." I have already explained my reasons for sharing the more common opinion that Corinthian "tongues" were not real languages, and that therefore their "interpretation" cannot be understood as "translation" in the normal sense of the word. Paul clearly presents the interpretation of tongues as one of the charisms (1 Cor 12:10), a gift for which the tongue-speaker should pray

(1 Cor 14:13), and that not all should expect to have (1 Cor 12:30). What strikes me as the most illuminating remark that Paul makes about the interpretation of tongues is found in 1 Corinthians 14:5: "He who prophesies is greater than he who speaks in tongues, unless some one interprets, so that the church may be edified." In other words, while speaking in tongues by itself is inferior to prophecy, when combined with interpretation it is equal to prophecy, and performs the same function.

Does the modern experience of these gifts shed any light on the question? My impression is that, as it is experienced in the charismatic renewal, speaking in tongues followed by interpretation is best understood as prophecy in two moments. The speaking in tongues is a signal that the Lord has a word to say to the group, and the interpretation is the word that the Lord wishes the group to hear. It is received and spoken in the same way that a prophecy is received and spoken.

One might ask: if the "interpretation" is really the same as a prophecy, what is the point of having it preceded by the speaking in tongues? In my opinion, the reason for this is that the prior speaking in tongues creates an atmosphere of intense inner listening, of expectancy for a word from the Lord. It alerts those in the group who prophesy to be ready to receive an inspiration as to what the Lord wants the group to hear, and it alerts the whole group to be ready to hear it. Of course, this explanation of tongues with interpretation takes for granted that there is not the kind of correspondence between the tongue-speech and the message that follows, such as would be the case if interpretation of tongues were really translation.

In my experience of prayer meetings it is a comparatively rare occurrence for someone to speak out in tongues in a way that calls for interpretation. Almost all of the use of tongues in prayer meetings will take place during times of spontaneous prayer, when everyone is praising God aloud in his or her own way, some with real words, others in tongues. This kind of prayer in tongues clearly does not call for interpretation. What does call for interpretation is the speaking out by one person in tongues at a time when everyone else is silent. In my opinion, tongue-speakers should not do this unless they are convinced that they are being genuinely inspired to do so. Before speaking out, they should seek confirmation in prayer that it is not just their own impulse, but that the Lord really wants them to do this. If they receive some such confirmation, then what they are equivalently saying to the group when they speak out in tongues is: "I believe that the Lord has something that he wants us to hear now, but I don't know what it is. Let's all listen for his word."

NINE

Charisms of Healings

A S WE HAVE ALREADY seen in our discussion of the Pauline lists of charisms, Paul never speaks of a "gift of healing," nor does he speak of any individuals as "healers." Paul mentions healing three times in 1 Corinthians 12 (vv. 9, 28, 30), and each time he uses the phrase *charismata iamaton,* which means "charisms of healings." The consistent use of this phrase suggests that Paul saw each healing as a charism, or gift of grace. But his statement, "To another [are given] charisms of healings," and his question, "Do all have charisms of healings?" suggest that when Paul talks about those who "have charisms of healings," he has in mind not the people who are healed, but people who are in some way involved in the healing of others. Paul's way of speaking of this implies that he does not see this as a habitual "gift of healing"; on the other hand, it does suggest that certain individuals are used with some frequency as channels or instruments of the healings that take place. If this is the case, then it would seem legitimate to speak of such people as having a ministry of gifts of healings for other people.

Actually, such a ministry was a very substantial part of the total ministry of Jesus, as it was also of the ministry of disciples. Let us look briefly at what the New Testament tells us about this.

The Healing Ministry of Jesus and His Disciples

To see how important a role healing played in the public life of Jesus, it will suffice simply to recall several passages in which the evangelists sum up the activity of Jesus in a few lines. We find two such summaries in Matthew:

> And he went about all Galilee, teaching in their synagogues and preaching the gospel of the kingdom and healing every disease and every infirmity among the people. So his fame spread throughout all Syria, and they brought him all the sick, those afflicted with various diseases and pains, demoniacs, epileptics, and paralytics, and he healed them.
> (Mt 4:23-24)

> And Jesus went about all the cities and villages, teaching in their synagogues and preaching the gospel of the kingdom, and healing every disease and every infirmity. (Mt 9:35)

Mark gives us a graphic description of the healings worked by Jesus:

> And when they got out of the boat, immediately the people recognized him, and ran about the whole neighborhood and began to bring sick people on their pallets to any place where they heard he was. And wherever he came, in villages, cities, or country, they laid the sick in the market places, and besought him that they might touch even the fringe of his garment; and as many as touched it were made well.
> (Mk 6:54-56)

Luke has a similar passage in his introduction to the sermon of the beatitudes:

> And he came down with them and stood on a level place, with a great crowd of his disciples and a great multitude of people from all Judea and Jerusalem and the seacoast of Tyre and Sidon, who came to hear him and to be healed of their diseases; and those who were troubled with unclean spirits were cured. And all the crowd sought to touch him, for power came forth from him and healed them all. (Lk 6:17-19)

Judging from the accounts of the public life of Jesus that have come down to us in the Gospels, it can hardly be denied that healing the sick played as large a role in his ministry as did teaching and preaching.

Furthermore, when Jesus sent out his disciples to preach the gospel of the kingdom, he shared with them not only his ministry of preaching, but his ministry of healing as well. We see this in all three Synoptics:

> And he called to him his twelve disciples and gave them authority over unclean spirits, to cast them out, and to heal every disease and every infirmity. . . .
>
> These twelve Jesus sent out, charging them, "Go nowhere among the Gentiles, and enter no town of the Samaritans, but go rather to the lost sheep of the house of Israel. And preach as you go, saying, 'The kingdom of heaven is at hand.' Heal the sick, raise the dead, cleanse lepers, cast out demons. You received without paying, give without pay."
>
> (Mt 10:1, 5-8)

> And he called to him the twelve, and began to send them out two by two, and gave them authority over the unclean spirits. . . . So they went out and preached that men should repent. And they cast out many demons, and anointed with oil many that were sick and healed them. (Mk 6:7, 12-13)

> And he called the twelve together and gave them power and authority over all demons and to cure diseases, and he sent them out to preach the kingdom of God and to heal. . . . And they departed and went through the villages, preaching the gospel and healing everywhere. (Lk 9:1-2, 6)

> Whenever you enter a town and they receive you, eat what is set before you; heal the sick in it and say to them, "The kingdom of God has come near to you." (Lk 10:8-9)

In the Acts of the Apostles, Luke seems to be at pains to balance the healing ministry of Peter, the hero of the first part of

Acts, with that of Paul, the hero of the second part. Thus, Peter heals the cripple at the temple gate (Acts 3:6-7); Paul likewise heals a cripple at Lystra (14:9-10). Many sick people are healed by Peter, even by having his shadow fall upon them (5:15-16); so also many are healed by Paul, even by the use of cloths that had touched his body (19:11). Peter raised a dead woman to life (9:40); Paul raised the young man who had fallen from the window (20:10).

Others besides the apostles shared the ministry of healing; thus we hear of the signs which accompanied the preaching of Philip in Samaria:

> And the multitudes with one accord gave heed to what was said by Philip, when they heard him and saw the signs which he did. For unclean spirits came out of many who were possessd, crying out with a loud voice; and many who were paralyzed or lame were healed. So there was much joy in that city. (Acts 8:6-8)

Most likely the "great wonders and signs" done by Stephen (Acts 6:8) included the healing of the sick also.

From the Letter of James (5:14-16) we learn that praying over the sick and anointing them with oil in the name of the Lord was part of the ministry of the elders of the church. This ministry was performed in the expectation that "the prayer of faith would save the sick man, and the Lord would raise him up." All the faithful were urged as well: "Pray for one another, that you may be healed."

I have already quoted a passage from the writings of St. Irenaeus which shows that gifts of healings were a matter of experience in the church toward the end of the second century. Speaking of the various gifts which were given to the church, he testifies, "Others heal the sick by laying their hands on them and they are made whole."

In the fifth century St. Augustine gives a striking testimony to the fact that healings of an extraordinary nature were still taking place in answer to prayer. In some earlier writings he had expressed the opinion that the age of miracles had passed; but after several years of pastoral experience as Bishop of Hippo he retracted his earlier view, and testified that in his own diocese alone, in a two-year period, nearly seventy well-attested miracles of healing had taken place.[1] He wrote:

Actually, if I kept merely to miracles of healing and omitted all others, and if I told only those wrought by this one martyr, the glorious St. Stephen, and if I limited myself to those that happened here at Hippo and Calama, I should have to fill several volumes, and even then I could do no more than tell those cases that have been officially recorded and attested for public reading in the churches. This recording and attesting, in fact, is what I took care to have done, once I realized how many miracles were occurring in our own day and which were so like the miracles of old and also how wrong it would be to allow the memory of these marvels of divine power to perish from among our people. It is only two years ago that the keeping of records was begun here in Hippo, and already, at this writing, we have nearly seventy attested miracles. I know with certain knowledge of many others which have not, so far, been officially recorded.[2]

It is not my intention to attempt even to sketch the history of the Christian experience of healing in answer to prayer. For my purpose it suffices to know that the Catholic tradition has always included the belief that, in answer to prayer, God can and sometimes does grant healings that surpass what one could expect normally to happen. This belief has been confirmed by the experience of such healings in every age of the church's history. It is true that in the course of time, prayer for healing, and the expectant faith that such prayer would be answered, came to be associated very closely, if not exclusively, with the invocation of saints, the veneration of their relics, and pilgrimages to shrines where relics were kept or apparitions had taken place. In the passage which we have just quoted from St. Augustine, we see that this was already the case in the fifth century, when there was a great flowering of devotion to the martyrs.

Unfortunately, in the course of the centuries, there was also a gradual obscuring of the meaning of the anointing of the sick, which eventually came to be seen as the "last sacrament," given to prepare the soul for death and judgment, rather than as a sacrament of healing for both body and soul. As a result, this anointing was usually administered without expectant faith that "the prayer of faith would save the sick man" or that "the Lord would raise him up" from his illness.[3] However, the liturgical renewal of our time has included the restoration of the full meaning of the sacrament of the anointing of the sick, and, it is to be hoped, experience of healings through this sacrament will strengthen the faith of the Catholic people in its efficacy as an instrument of God's power to heal the sick.

In the last decade, the faith of a great many Catholics in the efficacy also of non-sacramental prayer for healing has been awakened through their participation in the charismatic renewal. Prayer for the sick is certainly one of the most characteristic activities of any neo-pentecostal prayer group. During the prayer meetings there will usually be a period of intercessory prayer, which will almost always include prayer for the healing of sick people. After the prayer meeting, or at some other time, most prayer groups will provide an opportunity for those who feel the need of more prolonged and personal prayer to be helped by some members of the group who have demonstrated a particular gift for praying with people. Very often this will involve prayer for healing, whether spiritual or physical. A good many participants in these prayer groups learn how to be helpful to sick people by praying with them and helping them to pray.

What is most characteristic of prayer for the sick in the charismatic renewal is a lively faith in God's power to heal all our ills, whether physical or spiritual, whether they are judged normally curable or incurable. This faith is usually not the fruit of theological reflection, but rather of experience: both the experience of others, which is shared in the prayer meetings and through the literature of the renewal, and in many cases, of personal experience, whether of being healed or of witnessing the healing of another.

Obviously it is no one's experience that prayer for the sick is always answered with an extraordinary healing. On the other hand, there is enough experience of physical healings, even rather extraordinary ones, taking place after a sick person has been prayed over, to awaken and strengthen the faith of a great many Catholics in God's power to heal, and in his willing to do this in answer to the prayer of ordinary Christians like themselves.

In the case of a few people involved in charismatic renewal, the repeated experience of seeing extraordinary healings take place in people for whom they have prayed has led them to realize that God is calling them in a special way to a ministry to the sick. These are people who, in Paul's terminology, "have charisms of healings" (cf. 1 Cor 12:30). There is an analogy here with the gift of prophecy. As we have seen already, there is congregational prophecy, by which any member of the assembly may be inspired to speak, and there is the vocation of the prophet, by which a person is especially called to be the spokesman of God's word to his people. Similarly, there are the healings which happen occasionally in answer to the prayers of a group or some member of it, and there is the consistent pattern of healings through the ministry of certain individuals, which shows that this is their special gift and vocation from God. The analogy holds also in this respect: that as the vocation of the prophet does not confer the habitual power to prophesy (the prophet must wait for God's word to come to him), neither does the ministry of gifts of healing confer a habitual power to heal people (it is God who heals, when and as he chooses to manifest his power through this person's ministry). That is why, in my opinion, it is misleading to speak of such persons as "healers"— a term which, as we have seen, St. Paul did not use. On the other hand, it is evident from Paul's question, "Do all have gifts of healings?" that only certain individuals had such a ministry in the Pauline communities.[4]

The realization that they have been called by God to a ministry of gifts of healings has led some Catholics in recent years to conduct public healing services—something that until very recently would have been associated only with Pentecostals and some Evangelical Protestants. Francis MacNutt has conducted such services in many different parts of the world, helped by a team of Catholic religious and lay people who are also gifted for this kind of ministry.[5]

Some of these Catholic healing services have resembled those of Kathryn Kuhlmann and other Evangelical ministers, in that they have been marked by the phenomenon known as being "slain in the Spirit."[6] What happens is that some of the people, when they are being "prayed over," usually with the laying on of hands by the person praying, fall to the floor, and frequently remain for some period of time in a kind of trance, during which they are not unconscious, but their motor and sense faculties are diminished or seem temporarily suspended. MacNutt prefers to call this "resting in the Spirit"; his understanding of it is that "it is the power of the Spirit so filling a person with a heightened inner awareness that the body's energy fades away until it cannot stand."[7]

Now it surely comes as no surprise that the practices which I have been describing—prayer for healing, ministry of healing, public healing services, resting in the Spirit—encounter questions, doubts, skepticism, and even denunciation, on the part of many Catholics, even of some who on other accounts are rather sympathetic toward the charismatic renewal. I do not pretend to have the answer to all the questions that can be raised about charismatic healing. Nor is it my intention to attempt to justify all the practices which people involved in this ministry might engage in. For anyone who wants to read a full account and justification of this ministry, I recommend the books of Francis MacNutt.[8]

What I intend to do in the rest of this chapter is to offer to the reader the answers which I have worked out to some questions which this matter of healing has raised in my own mind. My questions tend to be theological rather than practical ones, and the answers will be of the same variety. I know, from talking about the charismatic renewal to various groups of people, that many others share the same questions that I have had about healing. I offer my answers in the hope that others will find them helpful.

How Is the Healing of Illness Related to Salvation?

The answer one gives to this question is inevitably going to depend on how one understands the significance of the healing ministry of Jesus. There is no need to repeat here what we have already said about the part that healing played in the total ministry of Jesus. One indication of this is the fact that nearly half of the Gospel of Mark is taken up with his narration of over twenty particular healings worked by Jesus.

When we reflect on the significance of Jesus' healings, it is obviously important to inquire how the evangelists themselves understood their meaning. As David Stanley has pointed out:

All the evangelists clearly regard them, not as a means of publicizing or accrediting the message of Jesus, but as an integral part of that message itself. That is to say, the evangelists are convinced that these acts of healing possess a profound christological significance far outweighing their "marvellous" character.[9]

In the synoptic gospels they are designated as "acts of power" (*dunameis*), a term which stresses their character as manifestations of the divine power, and hence their aptness, together with his words, as a vehicle of Jesus' proclamation of the coming of God's kingdom. They are presented simply as the good news in action.[10]

St. Luke, more than the other evangelists, has stressed the connection between healing and salvation. One indication of this is the way he consistently has Jesus speak of a person being "saved" when he or she has been healed. For instance, in the oft-repeated phrase which the Revised Standard Version translates "Your faith has made you well" (Lk 8:48; 17:19; 18:42), the Greek literally means "Your faith has saved you." Likewise, the promise which Jesus made to Jairus when it was reported that his daughter was dead, would literally be translated "Only believe, and she will be saved" (Lk 8:50). In each of these instances it is evident that it is the restoration of physical health which is being described as salvation.

It is typical of Matthew's Gospel that he sees the healings worked by Jesus as the fulfillment of Old Testament promises of salvation. This is particularly evident in the following passage:

> And when Jesus entered Peter's house, he saw his mother-in-law lying sick with a fever; he touched her hand, and the fever left her, and she rose and served him. That evening they brought to him many who were possessed with demons; and he cast out the spirits with a word, and healed all who were sick. This was to fulfil what was spoken by the prophet Isaiah, "He took our infirmities and bore our diseases."
>
> (Mt 8:14-17; cf. Is 53:4)

In the light of such passages as these, it is not surprising that in pentecostal and neo-pentecostal literature on healing, one sometimes finds an interpretation of the relationship between the healing of illness and salvation that tends to identify the two. One hears the argument, "Jesus took away our infirmities and bore our diseases just as truly as he took away our sins. Just as we should claim the forgiveness of our sins, by an act of faith, so all we need, in order to be healed, is the faith to claim our healing, which is already won for us by the saving work of Christ."

What is to be said of such a view? I find it unacceptable, for several reasons.

First of all, it would have disastrous consequences for anyone who accepts it, then falls ill and is not healed. We know that God sincerely wills the salvation of all people, and consequently offers to all the grace whereby they can be saved. If anyone is not saved, it is through his or her own fault. Now if the healing of illness were an integral part of the salvation wrought for us by Christ, it would follow that God must will the healing of the sick in the same way as he wills their salvation. Therefore, when sick people are not healed, it must be through their own fault; their failure to be healed shows that they lack the faith to claim their healing.

Now obviously, this would add an intolerable burden of guilt to the already heavy cross of unhealed illness. I find it impossible to believe that a premise with such consequences could be true. But I also have a more theological objection to it.

It seems to me that one could see the healing of illness as an integral part of the salvation wrought by Christ, so that we could claim healing with the same confidence with which we can claim forgiveness of our sins, only if one or the other of the following hypotheses were true: 1) if redemption meant the restoration of man to the state of original justice, or 2) if our redemption were already complete. But neither of these hypotheses is verified. Let us consider each of them in turn.

If "death came into the world through sin" (cf. Rom 5:12), it would seem that in the state of original justice we would not have been subject to death, and hence, presumably, not subject to the various causes of death, such as illness. Hence it would follow that if redemption meant our restoration to the state of original justice, the redeemed would also be freed from illness. But of course it is not true that redemption means our restoration to the state of original justice. The obvious proof of this is that we are still subject to death. Those whom Jesus healed, or even raised from the dead, still had to die, as all of us do. Again, we can look on the great saints as men and women who have most fully appropriated the salvation wrought by Christ. Their lives show that just as they had to struggle against temptation (and hence were not immune from concupiscence), so many of them had to contend with serious and chronic illnesses, from which their sanctity did not free them.

The other hypothesis, in which salvation would also mean

deliverance from illness, is that our redemption is already complete. Full redemption includes the "redemption of the body," which presumably would include the restoration of health. But, as St. Paul tells us, the redemption of our bodies is something for which we still have to wait in hope:

> We know that the whole creation has been groaning in travail together until now; and not only the creation, but we ourselves, who have the first fruits of the Spirit, groan inwardly as we wait for adoption as sons, the redemption of our bodies. For in this hope we were saved. (Rom 8:22-24)

This hope will be realized only at the last day, when "creation itself will be set free from its bondage to decay and obtain the glorious liberty of the children of God" (Rom 8:21).

In the actual order of redemption, death is the last enemy to be destroyed (1 Cor 15:26), and it will be destroyed by the resurrection of the dead, just as Christ's victory over death was not a miraculous descent from the cross, but his rising from the dead. During this present age, prior to the final coming of Christ, death is still a powerful enemy, over which the final victory of Christ is still awaited. But if death still has power over us, then our redemption is not yet complete, and the fact that we are redeemed and have "the first fruits of the Spirit" does not give us a claim to be free from the causes of death, such as infirmity and disease.

How then should we understand the relationship between healing and salvation, if we cannot accept the view that Christ has taken away our illnesses in the same way that he has taken away our sins? Let us look again at the Gospels, to see how the evangelists present the meaning of Jesus' healing ministry.

I can do no better than to follow the careful study which David Stanley has made of this question.

The first point to be noted is that the evangelists see the healings performed by Jesus as part of his campaign against the power which the evil one holds over mankind.

For Mark, the cures wrought by Jesus constitute the initial frontal attack upon the "kingdom" of satan. Jesus has come to inaugurate the establishment of the kingdom of God in history; and he must begin by breaking the hold of evil upon the world, liberating men from the thrall of "the strong man," satan.[11]

Matthew heartily endorses Mark's view of Jesus' work of healing as an important element in his campaign to destroy satan's "kingdom" upon earth.[12]

(In Luke) Jesus sees in these cures the preliminary defeat of evil.[13]

This view reflects the thoroughly biblical notion that sickness and death are consequences of sin, and hence manifest the power that Satan holds over fallen mankind. We find a striking expression of this in the words of Jesus about the crippled woman: "Ought not this woman, a daughter of Abraham whom Satan has bound for eighteen years, be loosed from this bond on the sabbath?" (Lk 13:16).

At the same time, we must note how carefully David Stanley has described Jesus' healings as the "initial" attack upon the kingdom of Satan, the "preliminary" defeat of evil. Healings do not constitute the total victory over death, which is yet to come. It is Luke who brings out most clearly the orientation of Jesus' healings to his future triumph:

In Luke's eyes, Jesus' "acts of power" in healing the sick are chiefly significant as pointers to his future lordship of the universe. . . . Jesus' miracles for Luke are primarily symbols of that salvation which "the Lord" will confer upon men.[14]

The key, then, to understanding the significance of Jesus' healings is to see that they point to a future victory over the power which death holds over mankind. They are real, and not merely conventional or arbitrary, signs of that future victory, because each healing of illness is a real, even though partial and temporary, victory over death. And death, in the biblical view, is not just a fact of organic life; seen as a consequence of sin, it is a manifestation of the power of Satan. Death is an enemy of God: indeed, it is "the last enemy to be destroyed" (1 Cor 15:26).

Jesus' healings, then, are "pointers to his future lordship of the universe." During the interval between the ascension and the parousia, Jesus is Lord at the right hand of the Father, and God is putting his enemies under his feet (cf. 1 Cor 15:25). But Jesus' lordship is not yet absolute and unopposed, because his enemies are still active and powerful; they will not be wholly destroyed until his final coming, when "death shall be no more" (Rv 21:4).

During this present time, each victory over death, even though partial and temporary, is nevertheless a sign, pointing to the total victory yet to come. Each healing of illness is a sign of that "redemption of the body" (Rom 8:23) for which we must still wait in hope. In brief, healing of any illness to which we are now subject is a real symbol of the ultimate salvation of our whole selves, body and soul, which will be accomplished only in our resurrection into eternal life.

Several consequences follow from this understanding of the relationship between healing and salvation. First of all, it explains why Jesus not only spent much of his public life healing people, but why he also sent out his disciples with power to heal, and why, in every age of the church, the Holy Spirit has continued to distribute "charisms of healings." The church, as Christ's body and bride, shares in his campaign against Satan, and the healings that are obtained through the prayers and sacraments of the church are signs, as Jesus' healings were, of the victory that he has already won over death by his own resurrection, and of the ultimate victory in which his church will share, when "the last enemy, death, will be destroyed" (1 Cor 15:26).

Second, in order for the healing of illness to be a sign of salvation, it is not necessary that everyone who is saved be likewise healed of any illness that he or she might have. Healing is a sign of the "redemption of our bodies," but it is not that redemption fully accomplished. It is still a valid and effective sign, even though we cannot count on its being given in any particular case.

For we have to keep in mind that healings in answer to the prayer of the faithful are charisms. It is the very nature of charisms that they manifest the sovereignly free and unpredictable working of the Holy Spirit. The Spirit is free to work such signs of the power of God to raise the dead in whom and through whom he chooses.

Jesus' own healings were also charismatic signs. He did not wipe out the diseases that afflicted and continue to afflict mankind: he cured the sick people whom he personally encountered in the course of a brief ministry in a very small part of the Roman Empire. His followers carried his message of salvation to the ends of the known world, and their preaching was accompanied by signs of Christ's lordship over the power of Satan, including the healing of the sick and raising of dead people to life. But neither did they wipe out sickness and disease from the world.

Understanding charismatic healings as signs pointing to a victory over death that is still to come helps us to accept the fact that some people are healed through prayer, and others are not. Each charismatic healing is a totally gratuitous anticipation of the "redemption of the body" which is still in the future. Being still subject to death and decay, we have no right, which we could claim before God, to be delivered from the causes of death, such as infirmity and disease. Charismatic healing is a foretaste of the resurrection of the body, which God now freely grants, when and where he chooses, as a sign of his power to raise the dead to eternal life. His sovereign freedom to work such signs in whomever he chooses is simply beyond any law by which we could predict who will be healed through prayer and who will not be healed, or by which we could grasp the mystery why one is healed and another is not.

Other Victories Over Death

To be healed of illness through prayer is a kind of victory over death, but it is not the only kind of victory we can win. For instance, martyrdom has always been hailed as a victory not only over the human tyrant, but over Satan and his reign of death. I would maintain that the patient acceptance of illness, especially when it seems that one is not going to get well, is also a victory of divine grace and the human spirit over death.

But getting well is also a victory over death, and this is true whether it is a case of charismatic healing or of healing through our natural vital powers, assisted by medical science. While healing in answer to prayer is a sign of God's power to raise the dead, we must not forget that God is intimately involved in every healing. Thomas Talley has put this very well:

> Thus all healing can be seen as an act of God, in that no therapeutic measure can have its effect apart from the dynamism of life itself. The practice of medicine is a dialogue with the life processes, not the simple manipulation of an inert material. And at the root of this life process there still resides the profound regenerative mystery which sustains the patient and the physician as well in humility and hope. There is no healing that is not an act of God.[15]

One conclusion that follows from this is that everyone who is involved in the healing arts and sciences (physicians, surgeons, nurses, researchers, etc.) is really on the side of God in the combat against death, the "last enemy," which God intends eventually to destroy. Here on earth we cannot gain the final victory, but every healing, and every advance in medical science, is a battle won in the campaign against the power that death holds over us.

It is obvious, therefore, that God wants us to have recourse to whatever medical help is available to us when we are ill, and that it would be presumptuous to refuse such help on the grounds that this would show a lack of faith in God's power to heal us. We have no way of knowing, in any particular case, whether God intends to work a sign of his power over death by healing us without medical help. The refusal of medical help is really a way of trying to force God to come up with a miracle—and this is not an attitude of genuine religious faith, but an attempt to manipulate God.

How Should We Pray for Healing?

We see in the Gospels that in many—but not all—cases, Jesus looked for faith in people before he healed them. The question he put to the two blind men most clearly tells us the kind of faith he looked for: "Do you believe that I am able to do this?" (Mt 9:28). It seems to me, in the light of this, that we should pray for healing, whether for ourselves or for another, with confident faith in God's power to heal us and, at the same time, with complete trust in his loving care for us. But I think it is a mistake to confuse such faith and trust, with confidence that God is going to manifest his power to heal in an extraordinary way, in any particular case.

Sometimes one hears the argument: "Jesus healed everyone who asked him with faith; therefore if we ask with faith we can be sure that he is going to heal us, too." The fallacy in this argument is that it does not take into account the unique character of the brief period of Jesus' public ministry, as a time for signs of the messianic kingdom breaking in and engaging the power of Satan. This time of personal encounter between Jesus as a man, still subject to pain and death, and his suffering fellow men and women was a never-to-be-repeated time in the history of the world. We cannot argue from the way Jesus healed everyone who came his way during those few years, to a law that would oblige him to heal all who ask for healing now, even if they have as much or greater faith than the cripples, lepers, and blind people who met him on the roads of Palestine.

Charismatic healings are totally gratuitous and therefore

unpredictable signs, and there is no way we can know that God intends to work such a sign unless he chooses to reveal his intention to us.

It does seem that sometimes God does reveal his intention of granting a healing in answer to prayer, so that a person could pray with confidence that God not only can but will heal this person. But apart from a private revelation to this effect, I do not see how one could know *how* God is going to answer prayers for healing. We can, of course, be sure *that* he hears and answers prayers that are made in faith. But, as I have already pointed out, there is more than one kind of victory over death.

Martha and Mary, beloved friends of Jesus, asked him to heal their brother Lazarus, and when Jesus finally came, each of them said to him in her grief, "Lord, if you had been here my brother would not have died" (Jn 11:21, 32). But we know from what followed that their prayer did not go unanswered; indeed it was answered beyond all their hopes when their brother came forth from the tomb. As Jesus had said to his disciples, "This illness is not unto death; it is for the glory of God" (Jn 11:4).

So, when we pray for healing, we do not dictate to God how he must answer our prayer. We should pray with absolute trust in his loving care for the sick person, but also with humble recognition of the fact that we do not know, any more than Martha and Mary did, what sort of victory over death will be for the greater glory of God.

Notes

Chapter One

1. Schema Constitutionis De Ecclesia (1963), n. 24; *Acta Synodalia Concilii Vaticani II*, vol. 2, pars 1, p. 259-60.

2. *Dictionnaire de Spiritualité Ascétique et Mystique*, vol. 2, p. 503-507.

3. A. Lemonnyer, O.P., *Dictionnaire de la Bible, Supplément*, vol. 1, p. 1233-43.

4. *Acta Synodalia*, vol. 2, pars 2, p. 629-30.

5. Leon Joseph Cardinal Suenens, "The Charismatic Dimension of the Church," in *Council Speeches of Vatican II*, ed. Y. Congar, H. Küng, D.O'Hanlon, London/New York, 1964, pp. 18-21. It has also been published in L.J. Suenens, *Coresponsibility in the Church*, New York, 1968, p. 214-18.

6. *Ibid.*, p. 214.

7. *Ibid.*, p. 215.

8. *Ibid.*, p. 216-17.

9. *Acta Synodalia*, vol. 2, pars 3, p. 504-505.

10. Dogmatic Constitution on the Church, "Lumen gentium," n. 12.

11. 1 Corinthians 13:3—"If I give away all I have, and if I deliver my body to be burned, but have not love, I gain nothing."

12. Yves Congar, O.P., *Lay People in the Church*, London, 1957, chap. 7.

13. Karl Rahner, S.J., *The Dynamic Element in the Church*, Freiburg/London, 1964, chap. 2. The original German edition was published in 1958.

Chapter Two

1. I do not include the letters to Timothy and Titus among the certainly authentic letters of St. Paul.

Chapter Three

1. J. Ruef, *Paul's First Letter to Corinth*, Penguin, 1971, p. 140f.; G. Iber, "Zum Verständnis von I Kor. 12.31," *Zeits. f. Nt. Wiss.* 54 (1963) 43-52.

2. Bruce Yocum, *Prophecy*, Servant Books, Ann Arbor, Mich., 1976, p. 146-48.

3. James D.G. Dunn, *Jesus and the Spirit*, SCM Press, London, 1975, p. 211.

Chapter Four

1. Vatican II, Decree on Ecumenism, n. 3.

2. Decree on Ecumenism, n. 4.

3. Yves Congar, O.P., "Charismatiques—ou quoi?" *La Croix*, Jan. 19, 1974, p. 10-11.

4. Vinson Synan, *The Holiness-Pentecostal Movement in the United States*, Eerdmans, Grand Rapids, Mich., 1971, p. 36. Late 19th-century revivalist preachers not of the Holiness movement were also using this term; see R.A. Torrey, *The Baptism with the Holy Spirit*, Chicago, 1895.

5. Vinson Synan, *Charismatic Bridges*, Servant Books, Ann Arbor, Mich., 1974, p. 8.

6. P. Damboriena, S.J., *Tongues as of Fire: Pentecostalism in Contemporary Christianity*, Corpus Bks., Washington/Cleveland, 1969, p. 155, 158, 162.

7. Kilian McDonnell, O.S.B., *Charismatic Renewal and the Churches,* Seabury, New York, 1976, p. 41-78, and more recently in *Presence, Power, Praise: Documents on the Charismatic Renewal,* Collegeville, 1980, vol. I, pp. lvi-lix. This is a 3-volume collection of practically all the statements that have been issued by church authorities concerning the charismatic renewal.

8. David Wilkerson, *The Cross and the Switchblade,* Pillar Bks., Westwood, N.J., 1964, and John Sherrill, *They Speak With Other Tongues,* Pyramid, New York, 1965.

9. For the early history of this movement among Catholics see Kevin and Dorothy Ranaghan, *Catholic Pentecostals,* Paulist, Paramus, N.J., 1969, and Edward O'Connor, C.S.C., *The Pentecostal Movement in the Catholic Church,* Ave Maria Press, Notre Dame, Ind., 1971, p. 13-107.

Chapter Five

1. *Theological and Pastoral Orientations on the Catholic Charismatic Renewal,* Servant Books, Ann Arbor, Mich., 1974.

2. *Ibid.,* p. 30.

3. *Ibid.,* p. 31.

4. Mark 1:8; John 1:33.

5. Matthew 3:11; Luke 3:16.

6. See P. Van Imschoot, "Baptême d'eau et baptême d'Esprit Saint," *Eph. Theol. Lov.* 13 (1936) 653-666.

7. Isaiah 32:15f.; 44:3f.; Ezekiel 36:26, 39:29; Joel 2:28f.

8. Acts 1:5 and 11:16.

9. Isaiah 32:15; 44:3; Ezekiel 39:29; Joel 2:28f.; Acts 2:17; 2:33; 10:45; Titus 3:6.

10. Luke 24:49; Acts 1:8; 2:4, 17, 33; 10:44, 45, 47; 11:15, 17.

11. *Theological and Pastoral Orientations,* p. 42.

12. *Summa Theologiae* I, q.43, a.6—"Sic ergo in eo ad quem fit missio, oportet duo considerare: scilicet inhabitationem gratiae, et innovationem quamdam per gratiam. Ad omnes ergo fit missio invisibilis, in quibus haec duo inveniuntur."

13. *Summa Theologiae* I, q.43, a.6, ad 2um.

14. *I Sent.* d.15, q.5, a.1, sol.2.

15. *Summa Theologiae* I, q.43, a.5, ad 2um.

16. *The Spiritual Exercises of St. Ignatius,* n. 15 (Annotation 15). I quote the translation by Louis J. Puhl, S.J. St. Paul Publications, Bombay, 1962.

17. *Ibid.*, n. 330 (Rules for the Discernment of Spirits, Rules for the Second Week, 2).

18. Acts 2:33.

19. French-speaking Catholics in the charismatic renewal use the term *l'effusion de l'Esprit,* and Italians use *l'effusione dello Spirito.*

Chapter Six

1. Dogmatic Constitution on the Church, n. 12.

2. See the titles mentioned above in note 9 to chapter 4.

3. Dogmatic Constitution on the Church, n. 30.

Chapter Seven

1. *Dogmatic Constitution on the Church,* n. 12.

2. *Ibid.,* n. 35.

3. J. Reiling, *Hermas and Christian Prophecy. A Study of the Eleventh Mandate,* Leiden, 1973, p. 10; also "Prophecy, the Spirit and the Church," in J. Panagopoulos, ed., *Prophetic Vocation in the New Testament and Today,* Leiden, 1977, p. 67.

4. T. Sota, 13:2.

5. *Jesus and the Spirit,* p. 229 (emphasis in the original).

6. *Jesus and the Spirit,* p. 234.

7. *The Didache,* 11:8-10; translation by R.A. Kraft, in *The Apostolic Fathers, A New Translation and Commentary,* vol. 3, New York, 1965, p. 170-71.

8. *The Shepherd of Hermas,* 11:7-16; translation by G.F. Snyder in *The Apostolic Fathers, A New Translation and Commentary,* vol. 6, Camden, 1968, p. 87-88.

9. *Didache,* 11:7.11, Kraft, p. 170-71.

10. *Ibid.,* 10:7, Kraft, p. 169.

11. *Ibid.,* 13:1-4, Kraft, p. 172.

12. *Ibid.,* 15:1-2, Kraft, p. 174.

13. *Hermas and Christian Prophecy,* p. 124-25.

14. *Ibid.,* p. 135-36.

15. *Dialogue with Trypho,* 82, translation in *The Fathers of the Church,* vol. 6, New York, 1948, p. 278.

16. *Hermas and Christian Prophecy,* p. 10.

17. St. Irenaeus, *Adversus Haereses* II, 32, 4; PG 7, 828-29; translation in *Ante-Nicene Christian Library,* vol. 5, p. 245-46.

18. *Adversus Haereses* III, 11, 9; PG 7, 890-91; translation in *Ante-Nicene Christian Library,* vol. 5, p. 295-96.

19. For a recent discussion of Montanism and the anti-Montanist polemic, see James Ash, "The Decline of Ecstatic Prophecy in the Early Church," *Theol. Stud.* 37 (1976) 227-52.

20. Eusebius, *Historia Ecclesiastica* V, 17, PG 20, 474-75; translation in *The Fathers of the Church,* vol. 19, 1, New York, 1953, p. 321.

21. James Ash, *art. cit.* p. 248-52.

22. George T. Montague, S.M., *The Spirit and His Gifts,* Paulist, New York, 1974, p. 46.

23. George Every, "Prophecy in the Christian Era," in *New Heaven, New Earth: An Encounter with Pentecostalism*, London, 1976, p. 161-206.

Chapter Eight

1. This chapter contains some of the material previously published in my article "Speaking in Tongues," *Lumen Vitae* 31, 1976, p. 145-70.

2. J. Kremer, *Pfingstbericht und Pfingstgeschehen*, Stuttgart, 1973, p. 165f.

3. On the probability of this opinion, see Kremer, *Pfingstbericht*, p. 251-53; R. Le Déaut, "Pentecost and Jewish Tradition," *Doctrine and Life* 20 (1970) 250-67; E. Haenchen, *The Acts of the Apostles*, p. 174; J. Potin, *La Fête Juive de la Pentecôte* (Lectio Divina 65), Paris, 1971, vol. 1, pp. 299-314.

4. *The Acts of the Apostles*, p. 189.

5. See J.G. Davies, "Pentecost and Glossolalia," *Jo. Th. St.* 3 (1952), p. 228-31; R.H. Gundry, "Ecstatic Utterance (NEB)?" JTS 17 (1966), p. 299-307; J.M. Ford, "Toward a Theology of 'Speaking in Tongues,'" *Th. Stud.* 32 (1971) p. 15-16.

6. See Hans Conzelmann, *First Corinthians*, Fortress, Philadelphia, p. 245; Huby, *Première Epître aux Corinthiens*, p. 340; Robertson-Plummer, *Int. Crit. Comm.* p. 321.

7. See footnote 5.

8. "Ecstatic Utterance," p. 306.

9. According to J.L. McKenzie, "The position of the city attracted a large and mixed population from the east; most of the citizens, it seems, were not Greek." *Dictionary of the Bible*, Macmillan, Milwaukee, 1965, p. 148.

10. G.B. Cutten, *Speaking with Tongues: Historically and Psychologically Considered*, Elliot's Bks., New Haven, Conn., 1927, p. 157.

11. E.B. Allo, *Première Epître aux Corinthiens,* 1956, p. 370.

12. *Ibid.,* p. 361.

13. *Ibid.,* p. 355.

14. See K. & D. Ranaghan, *Catholic Pentecostals,* p. 221.

15. Joseph Fichter, S.J., *The Catholic Cult of the Paraclete,* Sheed & Ward, New York, 1975, p. 62.

16. Fichter, p. 13.

17. Virginia B. Hine, "Pentecostal Glossolalia: Toward a Functional Interpretation," *Jo. Sc. St. Rel.* 8 (1969), p. 211-26; William J. Samarin, *Tongues of Men and Angels, The Religious Language of Pentecostalism,* Macmillan, New York, 1972.

18. He describes glossolalia as "patterned, improvised and incomprehensible speech" (p. 17); as "a vocal act believed by the speaker to be language and showing rudimentary language-like structure but no consistent word-meaning correspondence recognizable by either speaker or hearers" (p. xvii); and as "a meaningless but phonologically structured human utterance believed by the speaker to be a real language but bearing no systematic resemblance to any natural language, living or dead" (p. 2).

19. *Tongues,* p. 107.

20. "Pentecostal Glossolalia," p. 212.

21. *Tongues,* p. 119.

22. *Ibid.,* p. 127-28.

23. *Ibid.,* p. 122.

24. J.R. Jaquith, "Toward a Typology of Formal Communicative Behaviors: Glossolalia," *Anthrop. Ling.* 9 (1967), p. 1-8.

25. Jaquith, p. 6.

26. L. Christenson, *Speaking in Tongues and Its Significance for the Church,* Bethany Fel., Minneapolis, 1968, p. 116.

27. *Speaking in Tongues,* p. 28-29 (emphasis in original).

28. J.R. Williams, *The Era of the Spirit,* Logos, Plainfield, N.J., 1971, p. 32.

29. *Glossolalia,* Schloss Craheim, 1969, p. 18-19; also in his article "Et ils prient en d'autres langues, le mouvement charismatique et la glossolalie," *Foi et Vie* 72 (1973), p. 103.

30. W.J. Hollenweger, "Charisma and Oikoumene. The Pentecostal Contribution to the Church Universal," *One in Christ* 7 (1971), p. 332.

31. G.T. Montague, *Riding the Wind,* Servant Books, Ann Arbor, Mich., 1974, p. 45-47.

32. F.D. Goodman, *Speaking in Tongues, A Cross-Cultural Study of Glossolalia,* Univ. of Chicago Press, Chicago/London, 1972.

33. W.J. Samarin, "Variations and Variables in Religious Glossolalia," *Language in Society* 1 (1972), p. 123.

34. D.C. O'Connell and E.T. Bryant, "Some Psychological Reflections on Glossolalia," *Rev. for Rel.* 31 (1972), p. 975.

35. "Pentecostal Glossolalia," (see note 17), p. 212.

36. *Tongues of Men and Angels,* p. 33 (emphasis in original).

37. *Speaking in Tongues* (see note 26), p. 83f.

38. Published by Servant Books, Ann Arbor, Mich., 3rd ed., 1973. See pp. 146-52.

39. L.P. Gerlach and V.H. Hine, "Five Factors Crucial to the Growth and Spread of a Modern Religious Movement," *Jo. Sc. St. Rel.* 7 (1968), p. 32; also the same authors' book: *People, Power, Change, Movements of Social Transformation,* Bobbs-Merrill, Indianapolis/New York, 1970, p. 125. 1970, p. 125.

40. Aimé Solignac, "Jubilation," *Dict. de Spiritualité,* vol. 8, col. 1471-78.

41. Eddie Ensley, *Sounds of Wonder, Speaking in Tongues in the Catholic Tradition,* Paulist, New York/Paramus, 1977.

42. For examples of this, see Psalms 47:1; 66:1; 81:1; 95:1-2; RSV translates "make a joyful noise"; The New American Bible prefers "shout joyfully," or "sing joyfully."

43. *Enarrationes in Psalmos,* 32, ii, sermo 1:8, *CCL* 38, p. 254. For other text of St. Augustine on the same theme, see *CCL* 38, p. 161f; 533; *CCL* 39, p. 839; 1229f., 1332, 1374, 1394ff.; *CCL* 40, p. 1458.

44. Solignac, "Jubilation," 1476.

Chapter Nine

1. *Retractationes* 12,7; 13,5; translation in *The Fathers of the Church,* vol. 60. p. 55, 61f.

2. *De Civitate Dei* 22, 8; translation in *The Fathers of the Church,* vol. 8, p. 445.

3. James 5:15.

4. 1 Corinthians 12:30.

5. *The Power to Heal,* Ave Maria, Notre Dame, 1977, p. 9-10.

6. On this see G. Maloney, S.J., "How to Understand and Evaluate 'Slaying in the Spirit,'" *Crux,* Nov. 1, 1976, p. 1-8.

7. *The Power to Heal,* p. 203.

8. *Healing,* Ave Maria, Notre Dame, 1974, and *The Power to Heal* (see note 5).

9. David Stanley, S.J., "Salvation and Healing," *The Way* 10 (1970) 298-317; see p. 301.

10. *Ibid.,* p. 303.

11. *Ibid.,* p. 307-308.

12. *Ibid.,* p. 311.

13. *Ibid.,* p. 314.

14. *Ibid.,* p. 313-14.

15. Thomas Talley, "Healing, Sacrament or Charism?" *Worship* 46 (1972) 518-527; see p. 521.

Index